W9-AMP-424

The Pudding Hollow Cookbook

by Tinky Weisblat

Illustrations by Judith Russell

The Merry Lion Press
Hawley, Massachusetts

The Merry Lion Press
84 Middle Road
Hawley, MA 01339

Visit our web site at www.merrylion.com for information and recipes.

First printing 2004

ISBN   0-9742741-2-7

LCCN   2003116639

Cover by Dot2Design, Inc.

Printed in China.

Table of Contents

A Few Words of Introduction   *1*

Acknowledgments   *3*

Winter in Pudding Hollow   *5*
    soups, salads, stews, and breads to ward off the winter chills

Maple Time: The Fifth Season   *15*
    recipes to celebrate the joys and perils of mud season

Daffodil Days & Maybaskets   *25*
    reviving an old New England tradition

Learning from Rhubarb   *35*
    in praise of an unstoppable vegetable and two unstoppable women

An Early Summer Farm & Garden Tour   *45*
    a look at local agriculture and horticulture

Bountiful Berries   *57*
    taking advantage of summer's sweetest harvests

Playhouse Parties   *65*
    singing and eating at Singing Brook Farm

A Culinary Tour of Shelburne Falls   *77*
    a 19th-century village in 21st-century America

Listening & Eating with Mohawk Trail Concerts   89

        a unique chamber-music series and the foods it generates

Fair Weather Foods   99

        the satisfying cycle of fairs and fall festivals

Growing Older with Gourds   III

        learning to laugh with a copious food family

Why I Make Jelly   I2I

        What's a smart girl like me doing in a kitchen like this?

Judy & The Peaceable Kingdom   I3I

        remembering a folk artist who touched many lives

Humble Pie   I4I

        Charles Dudley Warner and the ultimate comfort food

The Pudding Contest   I5I

        a wholesome foodstuff and a useful legend

Index   I67

Looking for Paintings   *final page (174)*

Some Hawley Stars

A Bicentennial Gathering

A Few Words of Introduction

Pudding Hollow is a real place, a dip between hills in my hometown of Hawley, Massachusetts. It looks much as it does on the cover of this book, much as it has for more than two centuries. A few homes, the Hawley town office (a former one-room schoolhouse), and a cemetery mark its landscape.

Pudding Hollow is also a place of the imagination and of the heart. To me and to my late friend and collaborator, folk artist Judith Russell, the area in which I live and she spent her final years has long represented home in a sense that goes beyond the literal.

The ties hilltown dwellers feel here, to the land and to each other, constantly renew early American rural traditions that we value. Pudding Hollow thus serves as a metaphor for the best in New England life and country life.

A decade ago, Judy approached me with the idea of doing something called "The Pudding Hollow Cookbook." She announced that she had been inspired by Hawley's 1992 bicentennial pageant, in which a legendary 18th-century pudding-preparation contest was reenacted. The contest gave its name to the hollow in which the victor lived, and Judy and I both happily participated in the pageant.

Judy quickly painted the picture that graces the cover of this volume. In it she chose to blend the present and the past by blurring the reenactment and the actual contest. We still had no idea just exactly what a Pudding Hollow cookbook might be, however.

Slowly, I developed the ideas and Judy the art that make up this book. It describes our views–my "I" and Judy's "eye"–of the western hilltowns of Franklin County, Massachusetts (known collectively as West County), with special emphasis on Hawley. We decided to let the book by and large follow the rhythms of the year in our rural community, beginning with the season that dominates our landscape–winter.

Both scenerywise and foodwise, we had inspiring material to work with. Our countryside is lovely and serene; our mountains homey rather than daunting, lingering in neighborly fashion on the horizon. Our sky, unimpeded by city lights, is strewn with friendly stars at night. We are awash with color most of the year. Winter's dazzling white snow and blue-and-pink skies yield in turn to spring's hesitant greens and pastels, to summer's bright lights and brighter flowers and berries, and to the glorious New England autumn that has inspired poets.

Our relative lack of population helps preserve peace and quiet for humans and animals. Ironically, it also gives us a strong sense of community. The towns are small enough so that most of us know most of the others–and poor enough so that the majority of municipal tasks are performed by civic-minded amateurs rather than civil servants. We are proud of the area, its people, and its accomplishments.

We thought a cookbook was a particularly appropriate forum for showcasing the area because of the importance of food to the local landscape and people-scape. Despite relatively adverse soil and climate, we still have farmers among us. The hilltowns produce fruit, corn, maple syrup, potatoes, timber, and a variety of animals–cattle, sheep, hogs, poultry, and even llamas. Food is therefore not just something we buy in the store. We see it produced around us and remain tied to its seasonal patterns.

From their earliest days, the hilltowns have also depended on traditions of shared cooking and eating: food serves as a nexus of social life. Jams, jellies, preserves, and homemade mixes of one sort or another are a common gift, and we have plentiful, bounteous church suppers, bake sales, and seasonal festivals catered by traditional good plain cooks. Many use recipes handed down for generations.

Of course, this cookbook is more than just a tribute to Pudding Hollow and the ways of life it represents. Like much art and writing, it is autobiographical. Judy painted scenes that appealed to her because they reinforced her benign view of a world in which lions lie down with lambs and fields are always full of flowers. I tend to view recipes and places as keys to memory, and so I write not merely about food but about what it says to me about family, community, and nature.

Sadly, Judy died in the fall of 1994, after completing some but not all of the sketches and paintings for this book. Her family has supplied additional examples of her art, and friends have lent paintings to serve as illustrations. Readers will notice, however, that some chapters have more illustrations than others. I decided to leave the book this way rather than to seek out another illustrator who (however talented he or she might be) just wouldn't be Judy.

I'm sure readers will be as charmed by the art she left as everyone who met her was by Judy's talent and personality. Through the images she left, her spirit sheds a gentle, loving light on the annual cycle of growing, cooking, and eating in Pudding Hollow.

Acknowledgments

Many of the debts I owe are apparent throughout this book's pages as I name the numerous neighbors and friends who have shared their lives and their food traditions with me. A number of them died during the course of the book's assembly—most recently Ethel White, a strong and nurturing member of the West Hawley community, and Nancy Price, Judy's cousin and an early supporter of this project. As I pass on their recipes, I feel that I am lighting little candles in their honor.

I offer love and thanks to the memory of Judith Russell. I hope that her spirit is apparent in the book's pages. Judy's daughter Cara Morton has given me continued support as well as permission to reproduce her mother's images. I am further grateful to those who lent images to be photographed; besides Cara, these include Chris Burke, Bobbie Carlin, Rollo Kinsman, Joanne Potee, Patti Prunhuber, and Jan Weisblat.

Portions of this book have appeared in *American Profile, The Boston Globe, The Berkshire Eagle, The Daily Hampshire Gazette, The Shelburne Falls & West County News,* and *The Washington Post.* I thank those publications and their editors for helping me hone my prose.

Publishing a book was a new experience to me, one I could never have gotten through had it not been for the generous advice of colleagues. Special kudos are due to my publishing mentor, Bonnie Mickelson. Although a family crisis prevented her from publishing the book herself, Bonnie has cheerfully advised me on just about every phase of publication. I also appreciate the savvy lent to the project by my cover designer, Dot Lasky; my web designer and Photoshop tutor, Steve Hoffman; and my photographer, Will Elwell. All three have offered me more help than I could reasonably ask (or pay for).

I am enormously grateful to my three editors and testers—Jan Weisblat, Leigh Bullard Weisblat, and Peter Beck. Alice Parker Pyle and Judy Christian generously shared their superb proofreading skills as well. Any mistakes that remain are mine rather than theirs. Peter also served as design consultant, photographer, scanner, and sounding board for the project. He deserves to have his cookie jar filled forever.

I thank the friends and neighbors in both Massachusetts and New Jersey who tried dishes and offered comments. I feel blessed to be able to shop at Avery's Store; to sing at the Green Emporium and the Charlemont Federated Church; and to spend much of my life surrounded by the hills and community of Singing Brook Farm. I am especially grateful to my family members—Jan, Abe, David, Leigh, and Michael—for their resigned consumption of the results of my experiments, particularly when they longed for "ordinary" food.

This project has been funded in part by the Massachusetts Cultural Council as administered by the Charlemont/Hawley Cultural Council.

Winter in Pudding Hollow

Winter in Pudding Hollow

The beginning of the year in Pudding Hollow usually arrives in a blanket of snow. Our evergreens are flocked more thoroughly and more beautifully than those of any hopeful Christmas-tree vendor, and our hills resemble nothing so much as a holiday postcard. Our high latitude, with its low winter sun, forces the deep blue skies of midday to turn pink come afternoon. At night the winter moon tries to make up for the sun's dimmer rays by rising high in the sky and lingering luminously. Its shimmering reflection on the snow illuminates evening walks, recalling the story of Good King Wenceslas: "Brightly shone the moon that night, though the frost was cruel."

Winter in the hilltowns is a time for catching up. Writers like me tackle the long-term projects they have put off through months of busyness. Judy always painted up a storm. Other folk attack non-professional projects. My late neighbor Mary Parker, busy the rest of the year gardening and running a business out of her home, used the winter months as a reading vacation, immersing herself in the deeds of dead kings and queens as she perused historical works.

Another neighbor spends the long evenings quilting and crocheting, making gifts to present or sell at charity bazaars. A builder takes a break from fair-weather housing projects to construct wooden toys. His oxen, horses, and trucks delight children year round. Families watch videos and play games, hauling out old Scrabble sets and jigsaw puzzles.

Many puzzles–and projects–are never finished. To some, the snow-covered hills sing a siren's song. Cows, whose idea of fun involves low temperatures and little activity, savor their cool, cat-surrounded barn existence. Children go sledding and skiing, and humans and animals enjoy long treks in the snow.

My dog Truffle and I are lucky enough to live down the road from the Hawley State Forest, in which we find paths laid out by snowmobiles. Sometimes on our way into the woods we spot loggers at work, using oxen to tote remnants of trees down the hill. (Truffle is fascinated by the oxen but fortunately keeps out of the range of their feet.) While we walk, my cat Lorelei Lee amuses herself indoors staring through the window at the chickadees, finches, and cardinals snacking at a feeder.

Frequently, the weather forces us to stay indoors. On these days we make contact with others only via the telephone, for which we give thanks. A pot of warm soup on the stove can stretch indefinitely, and we're always happy to have leftovers to eat again and again–or to freeze in expectation of another storm. Quilts and afghans are gaily strewn about the house.

The recipes in this chapter are designed to replicate the feeling of winter. They smell tempting, taste satisfying, and linger in the stomach and memory. To those who hate the cold, they offer some compensation. To those who enjoy chilly weather, they complement the brisk cheeriness of the season.

Florette's Beef in Horseradish Sauce

This hearty dish resembles a pot roast; the horseradish and sour cream (plus the spices) will brighten your winter.

2 pounds top round or chuck
2 tablespoons oil
1-1/2 cups water (or beef stock, if you prefer)
1-1/2 teaspoons salt
(a little less if you're salt-conscious)
pepper to taste
1 onion, sliced
1 teaspoon curry powder
1/2 teaspoon ground ginger
1-1/2 tablespoons Worcestershire sauce
1 teaspoon sugar
1 cup sour cream
1-1/2 teaspoons horseradish
up to 2 tablespoons flour if needed

In a heavy pot or Dutch oven, brown the beef in the oil and add all the other ingredients except the sour cream, horseradish, and flour.

Cover the pot, and cook the mixture for 2 to 3 hours on a very low stove, checking on its progress from time to time. (A little more cooking will only make it more tender.) Just before serving, remove the meat, and add the sour cream and horseradish to the liquid. If the sauce is too thin, thicken it with a little flour.

Pour the sauce over the meat, and serve over cooked noodles or rice.

Serves 6 to 8.

Winter Corn and Tomato Soup

This flavorful soup is adapted from Herbal Soups *by Ruth Bass. If you like spice, use 2 cups of salsa and omit the vegetables. In either case, you'll feel you're tasting summer in mid-winter.*

2 cups fresh, frozen, or canned corn kernels
(or a bit more)
1 cup canned tomatoes
1 cup salsa
1 to 2 stalks celery, chopped
1/2 bell pepper, chopped
1 quart chicken or vegetable broth
(or a combination)
salt and pepper to taste
2 tablespoons butter
3 tablespoons flour
1 cup milk
grated store (Cheddar) cheese as needed
(about 2 tablespoons per serving)

In a large pot, combine the corn, tomatoes, salsa, celery, bell pepper, and broth. Add the salt and pepper, and simmer, covered, for 30 minutes or until the vegetables are tender. Cool the soup slightly, and puree it in small batches in a blender or food processor.

In a small saucepan, melt the butter and blend in the flour, making a roux. Gradually add the milk, and cook until thickened, stirring constantly. Add the milk mixture to the soup and stir well; then heat until it is just about to boil. Place the grated cheese in individual bowls, and pour the soup over it.

Serves 6 to 8.

Jan's Cordon Bleu Onion Soup

My mother Jan took a French cooking course in the early days of her marriage to my father and came home with a number of elegant recipes, including this hearty "soupe."

4 tablespoons butter
2 tablespoons olive oil
6 medium onions, sliced fine
1/2 teaspoon Dijon mustard
salt and pepper to taste
1 teaspoon flour
4-1/2 cups beef broth
1/2 cup dry wine, white or red (I prefer red)
toasted sliced French bread
grated Swiss cheese

Melt the butter in a large saucepan. Add the oil and the onions, and cook fiercely for a few minutes; then turn down the heat and continue cooking, stirring frequently, for about 30 minutes or until the onions begin to turn golden.

Add the mustard, salt, pepper, and flour, and stir the mixture until it is smooth. Slowly add the broth and the wine. Bring the mixture to a boil; then cover it, reduce the heat, and simmer for 20 to 25 minutes. Ladle the soup into crocks and top each with a piece of toasted bread and a generous smattering of the grated cheese. Place the crocks under the broiler until the cheese turns golden brown.

Serves 4.

Yankee Doodle Days White Chili

Every January, a crowd gathers at the Charlemont Inn for a chili cook-off. This popular meal raises money for Charlemont's annual summer fair, a three-day extravaganza known as Yankee Doodle Days. Appropriately, the chili funds are used for the purchase of fireworks. The cook-off spices up the winter doldrums of those who attend. "It's a highly charged event, much like the chile peppers it celebrates," says Marguerite Willis, who organizes the cook-off. This chili recipe, from John Lynch of Charlemont, is a perennial favorite at the cook-off. It is unusual in that it is a white chili—using no red meat, beans, or tomatoes. Its modestly spicy flavor (not to mention its aroma) always attracts a large group of fans.

1 pound Northern beans
2 pounds boneless, skinned chicken breast
1 tablespoon extra-virgin olive oil (plus a bit more if needed)
2 medium onions, chopped fine
4 garlic cloves, minced
2 cans (4 ounces each) chopped green chiles
2 teaspoons cumin seeds or ground cumin
1-1/2 teaspoons oregano
1/4 teaspoon ground cloves
1/4 teaspoon cayenne pepper
1 teaspoon salt (optional)
6 cups chicken stock

Soak the beans overnight. Remove and discard those that have risen to the top of the water, as well as any visible dirt and skins. Drain the remaining beans. Chop the chicken into bite-size chunks. In a frying pan, heat the tablespoon of olive oil. Sauté the onions, then add the garlic, chiles, and spices.

When the vegetables have wilted a bit, move them to a Dutch oven; then add a bit more oil to the frying pan if you need it, and quickly brown the chicken pieces. When they are brown, put them in the Dutch oven as well, and add the beans and chicken stock. Simmer the mixture, with the cover on but slightly ajar, for 2 hours over low heat, stirring occasionally.

Serves 8 to 10.

Uncle Jack's Sausage and Peppers

Like many of the best relatives, my late Uncle Jack wasn't actually blood kin. He and my mother met in their 20s and decided that they had so much in common—a sureness of themselves, a keen wit, and above all a lively sense of humor—that they must have been siblings accidentally separated in their early childhood. He loved to prepare this pungent pasta sauce with great fanfare and taught my brother David (who taught me) to make it. I think of them both whenever I prepare it. In many ways, it reminds me of Uncle Jack: uncomplicated on the surface, it is nevertheless full of zest and charms everyone who comes under its influence.

1 pound hot Italian sausage, cut into 1/2-inch pieces
1 pound sweet Italian sausage, cut into 1/2-inch pieces
2 jars (26 ounces each) of marinara sauce
3 to 4 bell peppers (any color combination you like), sliced
2 bay leaves
Italian seasonings (basil and oregano) to taste
3/4 cup red wine (not necessarily a great wine, but you may want to open a nice bottle and serve the rest with your meal)

In a frying pan, brown the sausage pieces. Transfer them to a large saucepan, and stir in the sauce, peppers, bay leaves, and seasonings. Drain off the excess fat, if any, from the frying pan. Then use the wine to deglaze the pan—that is, pour it in and use it to scrape up all the goopy bits on the edges of the pan—and pour it into the saucepan with the sauce mixture.

Place the saucepan over low heat, cover it, and simmer, stirring occasionally, for at least 2 hours. The sauce will be done when the peppers are soft and the flavors have blended.

This sauce tastes delicious over thick spaghetti, with shredded Parmesan or Romano cheese. It is even better when prepared a day ahead.

Serves 8.

Spinach Salad

Sometimes in the winter you're just dying for a salad–and lettuce is hard to come by. Here are a couple of alternative salads that work well with winter ingredients. The first is adapted from a salad served to me by Kathleen MacDonald, mother of my college roommate Amy.

enough spinach for 4 people (between 6 and 10 ounces, depending on appetite)
4 strips bacon
1 tablespoon red wine vinegar
1 tablespoon sugar
3 tablespoons mayonnaise
sliced red onion rings to taste

Wash the spinach carefully and drain it. Cut the bacon into 1/2-inch pieces and fry it until it is crisp. Discard all but 2 tablespoons of the bacon grease, and place the 2 tablespoons in a small saucepan. Add the vinegar, sugar, and mayonnaise to the bacon grease. Bring the mixture to a boil, and simmer over low heat until it is clear colored and slightly thickened. (If it is thick but not clear, give up and use it anyway; if you cook it too long, the mixture will curdle.)

Pour the hot mixture over the spinach, bacon pieces, and onions. Toss and eat immediately.

Serves 4.

Broccoli Salad

This recipe, from my seasonal neighbor Kat Fox Catts, takes advantage of the versatility of cold-weather broccoli. The salad takes a lot of chopping, but the effort is rewarded by the satisfying blend of textures.

1 medium bunch broccoli, cut up very fine
1/2 cup finely chopped celery
1/2 small red onion, chopped
1/2 cup raisins
8 slices cooked bacon, crumbled
1 cup mayonnaise
1/4 cup sugar
3 tablespoons red wine vinegar

Combine the first 5 ingredients. Whisk the remaining ingredients into a dressing, and toss them over the salad.

Serves 6 to 8.

Graham Biscuits

Winter main courses and salads cry out for warm, home-made breads. My sister-in-law Leigh and I adapted these biscuits from a recipe given to her by her friend Mary. The graham flavor gives them an extra-hearty texture. Like the graham bread in the maple chapter, these biscuits may be made with regular whole-wheat flour, but graham flour is an old-fashioned product that belongs in Pudding Hollow. If you can't find it in a local store, it may be ordered from the King Arthur Flour Baker's Catalogue (800-827-6836).

3/4 cup graham flour
2-1/4 cups white flour
2 teaspoons cream of tartar
1-1/2 teaspoons baking soda
1 scant teaspoon salt
3/4 cup shortening
1-1/4 cups buttermilk

Preheat the oven to 425 degrees. Mix the dry ingredients thoroughly in a bowl. Cut the shortening into the dry ingredients with a fork or pastry blender until the mixture resembles rice granules. Stir in the buttermilk. Knead the mixture once or twice in the bowl, then turn it onto a floured surface and knead a few more times. (Do not overhandle.)

Pat the dough out flat, then fold it over once. Knead it again two or three times. Pat, knead, and pat and fold again. (The folding will pay off when your biscuits come out of the oven with natural folds to hold butter.) The dough should end up about 3/4 inch thick. Cut it into biscuits with a biscuit cutter or a glass, and place them on an ungreased cookie sheet. Bake the biscuits until they turn golden brown (about 15 minutes).

Makes 12 to 18 biscuits, depending on the size of your biscuit cutter.

Elaine's Swedish Oatmeal Bread

Swedish-American Elaine Ostergren, who directed the choir at the Federated Church in Charlemont for many years, keeps the winter chills out with this hearty bread.

2 cups raw oatmeal
(Do not use instant!)
boiling water just to cover the oats
3/4 cup molasses
2 tablespoons sugar plus 1 teaspoon later
2 teaspoons salt
1 tablespoon shortening
2 teaspoons anise seed
1 egg, beaten
6 to 6-1/2 cups flour
1 package yeast

Cover the oatmeal (barely) with the boiling water. Add the molasses, 2 tablespoons sugar, salt, shortening, anise seed, and egg. Add 2 cups of the flour and mix well. Dissolve the remaining sugar in 1/2 cup warm water, and soften the yeast in it. Add this mixture to the other ingredients. Add enough of the remaining flour to make a dough that begins to hold together. Knead for 5 to 10 minutes, until elastic.

Place the dough in a greased bowl, and let it rise, covered with a damp towel, in a warm spot for 4 hours (less if using rapid-rise yeast). Punch down the dough, and shape it into 3 loaves. Place them in greased and floured loaf pans, and let them rise for another hour. About 15 minutes before this hour is up, preheat the oven to 325 degrees. Bake for 1 hour.

Makes 3 loaves.

Louise's Banana Cake

I include this cake in the winter chapter because one can buy bananas at any time of year–and because it is hearty and filling. Louise Gagnard, the mother of my graduate-school roommate Alice from Dallas, used to mail this cake to Alice and me whenever the winter blahs threatened to get us down. It makes me warm just to think about it!

1 cup (2 sticks) butter
2 cups sugar
2 eggs
1 teaspoon vanilla (optional–Louise didn't use it, but I tend to)
3 cups flour
2 teaspoons baking soda
1 pinch salt (also optional)
3/4 cup milk
4 to 5 ripe bananas, mashed

Preheat the oven to 350 degrees. Grease and flour a 10-inch bundt pan.

Cream the butter. Slowly add the sugar, then the eggs and the vanilla (if desired). Sift together the dry ingredients, and add them alternately with the milk. Add the mashed bananas, stirring to blend. Pour the batter into the pan.

Bake for 40 to 45 minutes, or until a toothpick inserted into the cake comes out clean.

Serves 12.

Maple Time

Maple Time: The Fifth Season

We New Englanders pride ourselves on our varied seasons. We revel in our springs of lilacs and daffodils, our deep-green summers, our spectacular fall colors, and our picture-postcard winters. In cataloguing these glories, we often forget the less glamorous fifth season that spans late winter and early spring.

Near my hilltown home in Hawley, mud season washes roads and yards in slush. Many of my friends and neighbors live on dirt byways and risk being mired in wet, viscous earth on a daily basis. Older residents remember that 50 years ago winter roads seldom proved unnavigable thanks to rollers that compacted the snow on road surfaces instead of clearing it. In contrast, the fifth season was a disaster for automobiles and even pedestrians. In those days country schools, open during the bleakest snowstorms, frequently closed down during mud season.

Now as then, despite the drabness of the landscape, the unseen beginnings of spring bring exhilaration to the air and herald a sudden burst of activity–sugaring off! Late night fires are spotted in sugar houses, and farmers buzz about tapping trees with sap buckets or plastic tubes. Their red faces, a product of the fires, give the illusion of an unseasonable sunburn.

Along with the sweet corn that flavors and colors our summers, maple syrup is our greatest culinary legacy from the Native Americans who originally lived in these parts. Maple syrup and maple sugar caught on with European settlers and citizens of the new Republic. They eventually proved to be a boon to abolitionists. These social reformers were reluctant to use molasses, with its ties to the slave trade, but also understandably reluctant to go without sweeteners altogether. Like today's maple harvesters, the early Yankees knew how much work it takes to reduce the clear sap to the dark syrup. Like them, too, they relished the tangy sweetness of maple syrup and sugar. Many part-time maple farmers admit that the syrup makes them very little money. It gives them occupation at a quiet time of year, however. And it provides them with a crop that doesn't need to be sold through a middle man; they can peddle syrup at roadside stands or (if they have the stamina and personnel) at sugar-house restaurants.

Judy's favorite among these restaurants, perched atop a scenic hill in Shelburne, belongs to Russ and Martha Davenport. When they decided to start a restaurant, the Davenports sought government seed money. They received it with the stipulation that they could sell only food they had grown themselves. For several seasons they did this full time, offering not merely maple breakfasts but also delicious filling lunches. Looking out the window to see a relative of the roast beef or chicken being served that day took a diner aback for a minute, but the food was so delicious–and so copious–that it was hard to stay disconcerted for long.

Lately, the Davenports have been able to open their restaurant only on weekends in maple season. In February and March it is well worth a visit. The family enhances the informal atmosphere of the sugar house and restaurant by inviting guests to explore the farm. I like to stroke the noses of calves (in their personal shelters, called "calftels") and to inspect the ever-hungry pigs on trips to Davenport's; the farm always seems to have a new litter of piglets pestering a tired but resigned sow. Chickens and rabbits happily beg for snacks. One gets muddy walking around Davenport's Farm in maple time, but the experience gives non-farmers a cleansing sense of agricultural rhythms.

For those unable to get to a restaurant like Davenport's, here are a few recipes to enable readers to savor the fifth season at home–to celebrate the magical time when sap yields to syrup and snow yields to crocus.

The Lure of Sap Time
from Ellene Scott

The Scott farm in East Hawley has been in the same family for over 200 years. It is one of the few working farms in Massachusetts to share that distinction. Matriarch Ellene is a spry woman with an offbeat sense of humor. Decades ago she came to Hawley from Ashfield "in the back of a truck, between a refrigerator and a couch." Although she knew no one in town when she arrived as a bride, she has become a native since.

I know a place in Hawley in God's great outdoors,
A quiet sheltered corner
On which the springtime pours
The wine of warmth and magic.
And well I know the sun
Has kissed the row of maples,
And sap begins to flow.

I want to see the bluebirds
And watch the sap snow fall,
To see the pussywillows and hear the robins' call;
To see the frisky chipmunks as oft before I've done.
I want to be in Hawley when sap begins to run.

I sit in seats of the mighty
And gather my share of the best.
Yet weary of toils that bring treasures,
Still now I am filled with unrest

Just ... because ... I want to see the sap bush
And smell the wood fire smoke,
And watch the boiling kettles
And see the old time folk.

I'm hungry for hot sugar
And the simple, homey fun
That's sure to be in Hawley
When the sap begins to run.

Maple Pea Baked Beans

This recipe comes from Martha Davenport, who reports that it was a Saturday night staple when her family was growing up and is popular with the Davenports even now. The beans it produces are delectably sweet.

1 pound Navy pea beans
1/2 pound salt pork
1/2 cup molasses
1/2 cup maple syrup (the darker the better; see note)
3/4 teaspoon Dijon or yellow mustard
1/8 teaspoon pepper
1/8 teaspoon paprika
1 teaspoon salt
1 apple, cored, peeled, and grated

Soak the beans overnight in cold water. The next day, rinse them, place them in a pot, and pour in water until it is an inch over the top of the beans. Cook the beans for 45 minutes to 1 hour, or until their skins get soft and crack. Pour them, and their water, into a 2-1/2-quart casserole dish or slow cooker (crock pot).

Fry the salt pork partially and drain it. Add it and all the other ingredients to the beans and mix well. The liquid should come to the top of the beans; add water if necessary.

Cover and bake at 300 degrees for 5 to 6 hours or cook for 10 to 12 hours in the crock pot.

Serves 6 to 8.

Note: When you buy maple syrup from the farm (as opposed to the supermarket), you usually have a choice of grades, from fancy and A (very light, very delicate) to blackstrap (the darkest of them all). The grading depends on the weather, the sap, and the farmer's choice. Some people prefer grade A for eating on pancakes, while others prefer the stronger taste of lower grades. All agree that darker syrup is best for cooking, however.

Vermont Pork Chops

Despite its name, this recipe comes from the Massachusetts Maple Producers Association, an organization that is headed up by Tom McCrumm in the West County town of Ashfield. It makes a lovely sweet-and-sour main dish.

6 pork chops
canola or extra-virgin olive oil as needed for browning
1/4 cup chopped onion
1 tablespoon cider vinegar
1/2 teaspoon chili powder
1/2 teaspoon pepper
1/4 cup maple syrup
1/4 cup water
1 tablespoon Worcestershire sauce
1-1/2 teaspoons salt
flour as needed to thicken the gravy

Preheat the oven to 400 degrees. Lightly brown the pork chops in a small amount of oil; then place them in a 9-by-13-inch baking dish. Combine the other ingredients except the flour over low heat, and pour them over the chops. Cover and bake for 45 minutes, basting occasionally. Uncover and bake for 15 more minutes.

Place the pork chops on a warming platter, and pour the sauce into a saucepan. Thicken it slightly with flour to make a gravy, and serve it over the chops. Serves 4 to 6, depending on the size of your pork chops.

Maple Red Cabbage

This is my mother's adaptation of classic red cabbage. She insists on the vinegar, but I prefer to concentrate on the maple and cabbage. Either way, the dish is full of color and flavor.

5 slices bacon, minced
1 small onion, chopped
1 Granny Smith apple, peeled, cored, and sliced thin
6 cups red cabbage, shredded
1/2 cup maple syrup
1/2 cup water
4 teaspoons cider vinegar (optional)
1/2 teaspoon caraway seed
salt and pepper to taste

Fry the bacon pieces until almost crisp. Add the chopped onion, and sauté until the onion is translucent. Pop the bacon and onion into a saucepan with the remaining ingredients. Bring the mixture to a boil, reduce the heat, cover, and cook slowly for at least 45 minutes, stirring occasionally.

Serves 4 to 6.

Maple Pickled Beets

Here's another recipe from Martha Davenport. The smaller your beets are, the more you will be able to fit into your rosy jars. The quantities of syrup and vinegar are approximate and will vary slightly with the size of your beets. You may increase the ingredients proportionally to use more beets. If you decide to use quart jars, however, process them for 30 minutes.

small beets, cooked and peeled, as needed to fit into 2 pint jars
3/4 cup maple syrup
3/4 cup cider vinegar
1/4 teaspoon (scant) Kosher salt

Pack the beets into sterile jars, filling the jars to within 1/2 inch of the tops. Combine the remaining ingredients in a saucepan. Bring them to a boil, pour over the beets, and seal. Process for 20 minutes. (See "About Processing," page 123.) Makes 2 pints.

Maple-Balsamic Vinaigrette

My neighbor John Cosby inspired me to experiment with this salad dressing. Everyone who has tried it approves. Feel free to adapt it to your palate.

4 tablespoons balsamic vinegar
4 tablespoons maple syrup
1 clove garlic, minced
1/4 teaspoon Dijon mustard
2 tablespoons water
1/2 teaspoon salt
pepper to taste
1 cup extra virgin olive oil

In a bowl, combine all the ingredients except the oil. Then slowly whisk in the oil. This dressing may be kept in the refrigerator for up to a month. Just be sure to bring it to room temperature and shake it before serving.

Makes about 1-1/2 cups.

Quick Graham Bread

Here's a recipe from my neighbor Ethel White that uses graham flour–a whole-wheat variation that is much neglected in modern cooking, in my opinion. If you can't find graham flour, feel free to substitute regular whole-wheat flour. Because of its coarser consistency, however, graham flour is worth seeking out. It may be ordered from the King Arthur Flour Baker's Catalogue (800-827-6836). Ethel says she learned to make this bread when she was nine. "When my youngest brother was born, a practical nurse came and took care of my mother," she explains. "The baby was born at home. And this woman taught me how to make this bread." Actually, Ethel's original recipe called for molasses, which you may certainly use. The maple syrup works beautifully, however.

1/4 cup sugar
1 teaspoon baking soda
1-1/2 cups graham flour
1/2 cup white flour
1/4 teaspoon salt
3 tablespoons liquid shortening (e.g., canola oil)
1 cup sour milk
(this can be created by adding 1 tablespoon of lemon juice or vinegar to regular milk and allowing the mixture to sit for 10 minutes)
1/2 cup maple syrup
1/2 cup chopped dates or raisins (optional)

Preheat the oven to 350 degrees. Combine the dry ingredients. Add the shortening, milk, and syrup. Mix gently but thoroughly. Stir in the dates or raisins, if desired. Bake in a greased loaf pan for 1 hour. Makes 1 loaf.

Pudding Chômeur

Canadian visitor Denis Carrier brought this delectable pudding with him when he visited my neighbors. Chômeur means "unemployed person," and Denis's sauce originally called for 1-1/2 cups brown sugar, 3 tablespoons flour, 2 tablespoons sweet butter, and 2 cups water. If you're employed enough to be able to afford maple syrup, however, you'll probably prefer this version.

for the sauce:
1-1/2 cups maple syrup
3/4 cup water
2 tablespoons sweet butter

for the cake:
1 tablespoon sweet butter at room temperature
1/2 cup sugar
1 egg, beaten
1 cup flour
1-1/2 teaspoons baking powder
1/2 teaspoon salt
1/3 cup milk

First, make the sauce: In a saucepan, combine the maple syrup and water. Bring them to a boil; then remove the saucepan from the heat. Add the butter and set aside.

Next, make the cake: Preheat the oven to 350 degrees. Cream together the butter and the sugar. (This will take a bit of work as there isn't a lot of butter, but do your best.) Add the egg and mix well. Add the dry ingredients, alternating with the milk. Spread the batter into a greased, 8-inch-square pan. Pour the sauce gently over the batter. Bake for 35 minutes; the sauce will sink to the bottom, and the cake will firm up a bit. Serve as an upside-down cake. This is delicious with ice cream.

Makes 8 to 9 servings.

Sugar Eats

One annual event in the Pudding Hollow region invokes maple time months after the mud has dried up. Each July community members gather to eat maple sugar on snow at a sugar eat. Sugar on snow is maple syrup boiled to the soft-ball stage (234 degrees) and poured over fresh snow. It is the simplest and most devastating maple dish imaginable. Its gooey texture provides a lot of work for dentists. Nevertheless, most eaters of this sticky treat deem it worth the risk, although they often cut the sweetness of the syrup by eating pickles on the side. Sugar eats are a long-standing tradition in Hawley. Decades ago, townspeople would dig a big hole in the ground in the winter, pile snow into it, and cover the snow with sawdust. In the summer they would dig up the snow and eat it with maple syrup. Nowadays, they just use an ice machine. It's less romantic but also less work.

Maple Candy Corn

This treat makes an excellent hostess gift; it's tasty but not too heavy. Of course, you may nibble it up before you get to your hostess! Even though much of its sweetness comes from the sugar, the maple flavor comes through loud and clear.

3 quarts popped popcorn
1/2 cup (1 stick) sweet butter
1 cup brown sugar, firmly packed
1 cup pecans, halved (or chopped), plus a few more if you can't resist
1/4 cup maple syrup
1/2 teaspoon salt
1/4 teaspoon baking soda
3/4 teaspoon vanilla

Preheat the oven to 250 degrees. Place the popped corn in a greased roasting pan. Combine all the other ingredients except the baking soda and vanilla in a heavy saucepan. Bring the mixture to a full boil, stirring constantly. Boil for 2 minutes over medium heat. Remove the pan from the heat, and stir in the baking soda and vanilla. (The mixture will froth.) Quickly pour the syrup over the popped corn and mix thoroughly. Bake for an hour, stirring every 15 minutes. Remove from the oven and cool completely. Break into pieces and store in an airtight container for up to a week. (It never lasts that long!) Makes 3 quarts.

Maple Squares

I don't generally approve of using maple flavoring, which seems like cheating somehow, but I simply couldn't replicate these chewy bars with syrup. The recipe comes from my friend Charlotte Thwing, a spry 80-something year old with the gift of eternal youth.

2 eggs
1 cup white sugar
1/3 cup (2/3 stick) sweet butter, melted
1 cup flour
1 teaspoon baking powder
1 pinch salt
3/4 teaspoon vanilla extract
3/4 teaspoon maple extract
1 cup brown sugar, firmly packed
1/2 cup walnuts, chopped

Preheat the oven to 350 degrees. Separate the eggs. Add the sugar to the egg yolks and beat (as well as you can–the mixture will be a little dry!). Stir in the melted butter. Sift together the flour, baking powder, and salt, and stir them into the first mixture. Add 1/4 teaspoon of each extract. Place in a greased 6-by-10-inch (or 8-by-8-inch) pan. Beat the egg whites until they are stiff, and fold in the remaining ingredients, including the leftover extracts. Spread this mixture over the top of the pan. Bake for 30 minutes. Cool and cut into bars. Makes 16 bars.

The Charlemont Inn's Cider-Maple Dumplings

This recipe comes from Charlotte Dewey of the Charlemont Inn, whose mother Jean invented the dumplings. Filling and sweet but not too sweet, they are one of the Inn's most popular offerings.

for the biscuits:
3-1/2 cups flour
1 teaspoon salt
2 tablespoons baking powder
3/4 cup (1-1/2 sticks) sweet butter
1-1/2 cups milk

for the liquid:
1 cup cider
1 cup maple syrup
1/4 cup (1/2 stick) sweet butter

Preheat the oven to 400 degrees. To prepare the batter for the biscuits, whisk together the flour, salt, and baking powder. Cut the butter in until the mixture achieves a mealy consistency. Add the milk all at once. Stir the batter with a fork just until it holds together, and toss it onto a floured board. Knead several times, and cut into 15 rounds, each about 2-1/2 inches in diameter. (A glass will do as a cutter.)

Combine the liquid ingredients and bring them to a simmer in an ungreased 9-by-13-inch baking pan in the preheated oven. Lay the biscuits on top and bake until they are light brown, about 20 minutes. Serve with ice cream or whipped cream. Serves 15.

Spring Swing

Daffodil Days & Maybaskets

We get pretty sick of waiting for spring in the Massachusetts hilltowns, but the prolonged expectation seems worthwhile when nature finally cooperates. Patchworks of sprightly green magically appear on hillsides, and yardsful of daffodils and jonquils seem to raise their heads to the sun overnight.

The daffodil-bedecked beginning of May in Pudding Hollow always reminds me of the now defunct tradition of hanging Maybaskets in doorways. These small, hand-decorated baskets were a legacy of the old English habit of hailing May 1 as the first day of spring by spending the day "a-Maying" in the woods–gathering blossoms and tree branches and dancing around Maypoles.

Viewed as frivolous and pagan by Puritans, May Day was banned in England during Oliver Cromwell's reign. It's not clear when it crept back into the practices of Puritan New England, but the custom of celebrating it with Maybaskets (and occasionally Maypoles) was a popular one in many parts of Massachusetts up to two generations ago.

The holiday was celebrated in differing ways among various groups of New England children. Some children prepared Maybaskets only for their mothers. Others brought baskets full of flowers to shut-ins. Some felt they had to have the baskets in place by dawn. For others, the baskets could be delivered any time at all during the first day of May.

In Hawley, Maybasket giving was elevated to a community ritual that lasted all month long. My late neighbor Shirley Raymond McMullin, who lived in the Pudding Hollow district all her life, remembered that neighborhood children spent the month of May constructing small baskets "out of whatever–boxes, or paper, or construction paper; all kinds of things." She added, "With tissue paper and crepe paper, whatever we could do."

The children gathered spring flowers (mainly daffodils and violets) to put into the containers and badgered their parents to help them prepare sweets to stick in as well. After supper on each May evening they clustered in groups to hang that day's baskets on the door of one child (or occasionally one adult) in the neighborhood.

"The idea was," recalled Shirley, "we would choose the fastest runner to do the hanging because you put the baskets on the doorstep and knocked on the door and then you ran like crazy and hid. And whoever you were hanging on–of course you put your names on the baskets, so they knew who was there. And they had to come and find you, catch you. And then after you were caught, you sat on their doorstep until they had caught everybody, and then sort of had a party."

The experience of "hanging on" their neighbors brought these children together and crossed class boundaries: the baskets didn't have to be fancy. Shirley said of the boys in one family, "They did not have a lot of worldly goods. But they found the most lovely white violets, wild violets. And they were always so very fragrant. I always looked forward to that."

No one is quite sure what happened to the Maybasket tradition. Shirley speculated that perhaps it petered out as a result of the closing of the local one-room schools. When Hawley children began attending school with children in the next town, they lost both the sharing of the custom and the closeness of the neighborhood.

Today, as adults and children all over the United States renew their search for community, it seems to me that the habit of delivering Maybaskets is well worth resurrecting, on May 1 if not all month. Making baskets will nurture our creative impulses. Searching lawns and fields for wildflowers will help us savor nature's gifts. Creating the baskets' culinary treasures will foster the special adult-child interaction that cooking brings. And delivering the baskets will rekindle the notion of neighborhood.

Here are a few recipes for those who want to celebrate the daffodil days with baskets full of good will.

Daffodil Days

Buckeyes

Children love to make this simple recipe. Adults may find the resulting product incredibly sweet, but I've never met a child who viewed oversweetness as a problem. Catherine Newell of Charlemont, who provided the recipe, melts a small bit of paraffin wax (about 1/2 teaspoon) with the chocolate to smooth out the balls. I have tried the recipe with the paraffin, but it works very well without.

1 cup peanut butter

1/2 cup (1 stick) sweet butter, at room temperature

2-3/4 cups confectioner's sugar

12 ounces semi-sweet chocolate chips or cut-up milk chocolate

(according to preference; my young nephew Michael likes to use some of each and have two different flavors of buckeyes)

Cream the peanut butter and butter together, and add the confectioner's sugar. Form into 3/4-inch balls, and refrigerate for at least 2 hours. Melt the chocolate over a double boiler. Put toothpicks into the peanut-butter balls. Dip the balls in the melted chocolate mixture. (Be careful to pace yourself, or you'll have to melt more chocolate!) Leave an undipped space around each toothpick so the confection resembles a buckeye. Place the candies on waxed paper and refrigerate until firm. Makes 3 to 4 dozen.

Penuche

This fudge fools recipients into thinking it has a maple base. As a child, my neighbor Harrison Parker was so enamored of it that he dubbed his wooden boat the "S.S. Sour Cream Penuche" and sailed around the family pond with a piece of fudge perched on each corner of the craft. I'd rather eat it than sail it, but it is worthy of commemoration.

1 cup sour cream

1 pound brown sugar

1 cup white sugar

1 teaspoon vanilla

1 cup chopped walnuts or pecans (optional)

In a heavy saucepan combine the sour cream and sugars. Cook over medium heat, stirring frequently, to the soft-ball stage (234 degrees). Be careful not to overcook the fudge. Be careful not to undercook it, either, or it won't set!

Remove the fudge from the heat, and stir in the vanilla. Beat the fudge with a wooden spoon. This may take up to 15 minutes. The moment it starts to change from glossy to creamy, add the nuts if desired (they cut the sweetness of the fudge), and pour the confection into a greased 9-by-9-inch pan. Cut into 25 pieces when cool.

U.S.S. SOUR CREAM PENUCHY · HAWLEY

Cream Candy

Kathryn Scott Flagg, a frequent contributor to the newsletter The Edge of Hawley, *has written that cream candy was a popular addition to Maybaskets in her childhood. If you've never had cream candy, you're in for a treat; it literally melts in your mouth. Unfortunately, this sweet is temperamental: it can't be made on a humid day, it seems to take forever to cook, and it turns into a mess if you stop pulling it once you've started. (Be sure to have lots of pullers on hand–optimally, four–for the ten minutes or so the pulling takes.) It's worth the pains it takes. Note that you MUST wait a day before eating this candy. It's while cooling and resettling that the confection crystallizes and "creams."*

4 cups sugar
1 cup water
1/8 teaspoon baking soda
1/2 teaspoon salt
1 cup heavy cream
a few drops of vanilla extract

Directions:

Combine the sugar, water, soda, and salt in a large Dutch oven. (I use my big soup pot; this stuff really rises while cooking!) Cook over medium heat, stirring constantly, until the sugar dissolves. Cover the pot, and continue to cook for 2 to 3 minutes. (Covering washes the sugar crystals down from the sides of the pan.) Uncover the mixture, and cook, without stirring, until it reaches the soft-ball stage (234 degrees).

Slowly trickle the cream into the hot liquid. Do not stir. Continue to cook over medium heat until the mixture reaches the hard-ball stage (260 degrees.)

Remove the pan from the heat. Pour the mixture onto a well buttered marble slab (or divide it onto 2 slabs so 2 people can work on it at once). Be sure not to scrape the candy mixture from the bottom of the pan. Although marble is always cooler than the air surrounding it, it helps if you have cooled your slabs even further by placing filled ice-cube trays on them while the candy is cooking.

Dribble the vanilla onto the cooling candy. (It will mix in as you pull.) Then push the mixture into a mound with a buttered spatula or candy scraper. As soon it is cool enough to touch, lift it up with buttered hands (which you continue to re-butter as you go along to avoid burning them and to keep the candy fluid). Pull, twist, and fold the candy until it becomes opaque and starts to stiffen. Divide the candy in half (or divide each mound in half), and pull each section into a rope that measures about 1/2 inch in diameter. Cut each rope into 1-inch pieces with scissors that have been cooling in the freezer. Wrap each piece in waxed paper, and store the candy in an airtight container at least overnight. Makes about 6 dozen pieces.

Black-Bottom Cupcakes

This recipe probably wasn't in vogue years ago as it's a recent phenomenon. Nevertheless, these treats would go well in a Maybasket; they aren't messy, and they're easy and fun for kids to make. The recipe comes from Karen Hogness, who with her husband Dennis Avery runs Avery's General Store in Charlemont–a lifeline to many of us in the hilltowns.

8 ounces cream cheese, at room temperature
1 egg
1-1/3 cups sugar
1/8 teaspoon plus 1/2 teaspoon salt
1 cup chocolate chips (6 ounces)
1-1/2 cups sifted flour
1 teaspoon baking soda
1/4 cup cocoa
1 cup water
1/3 cup canola oil
1 tablespoon vinegar
1 teaspoon vanilla
cupcake liners (about 24)

Preheat the oven to 350 degrees. Place the cream cheese, the egg, 1/3 cup of the sugar, and the 1/8 teaspoon salt in a mixing bowl. Beat well and stir in the chocolate chips. Set aside. Beat all the remaining ingredients until blended. Fill the cupcake liners 1/3 full with the flour mixture. Do not overfill; try to fill 24 of them! Top each with a heaping teaspoon of the cream-cheese mixture. Bake for 20 to 30 minutes.

Makes about 24 cupcakes.

Hawley Snowballs

This recipe for popcorn balls comes from my neighbor Ethel White, who made it frequently growing up and later for great-grandchildren. She obtained it from Clara Bicknell of Charlemont, who taught at the Pudding Hollow School about 70 years ago. The molasses gives the balls a robust flavor. I gave some to Shirley McMullin one winter, and she dubbed them "Hawley Snowballs."

1 cup molasses
1 cup sugar
2 tablespoons vinegar
sweet butter the size of a walnut
1 pinch baking soda
3 quarts popped popcorn

Combine the molasses, sugar, vinegar, and butter in a heavy saucepan. Bring to a boil and cook for 10 minutes, stirring frequently. Take the mixture off the stove, add the baking soda, and stir well. Pour over the popped corn. Quickly form the sticky popcorn into 2-inch balls with well greased hands. (If they're not well enough greased, you'll have clumps rather than balls.) Makes about 18 balls.

Gum-Drop Cookies

These cookies are another contribution from Ethel White. I make them at Christmas time with red and green gum drops, but they add color to any season. The cookies are yummy even without the drops. Beware: cutting up gum drops is sticky work!

1 cup (2 sticks) sweet butter at room temperature
1 cup white sugar
1 cup brown sugar, firmly packed
2 eggs, well beaten
1 teaspoon vanilla
2 cups flour
1 teaspoon baking powder
1/2 teaspoon salt
2 cups uncooked regular (not quick) oatmeal
1 cup coconut
1 cup fruit gum drops (or more), cut up

Preheat the oven to 350 degrees. Cream the butter, and add the sugars and eggs. Beat well. Stir in the vanilla. Sift together the flour, baking powder, and salt, and add them to the butter mixture; then add the oatmeal, coconut, and gum drops. Drop small spoonsful of the dough onto greased cookie sheets, and bake for 10 to 12 minutes.

Makes about 75 small cookies.

Glazed Pecans

These yummy nuts probably weren't in anybody's Maybaskets in days gone by. This recipe comes from Hsui-li Chen Kelley, a Chinese woman who married into a local farm family. The nuts should have a place in any future basket-hanging parties, however. They also make a terrific gift for people like my brother David, who appreciates edible offerings at any time, especially during the holidays.

3/4 to 1 cup white sugar (depending on your sweet tooth)
about 1/2 cup water
2 cups shelled pecans
1-1/2 cups oil for frying

Boil the sugar and water together in a saucepan until the sugar has dissolved. Add the nuts and boil, stirring constantly, for 10 minutes. Strain the nuts from the sugar water. Place the oil in another saucepan, small in diameter but deep.

Heat the oil to 325 degrees. Place the nuts in the oil and fry until they are light brown and you can smell them. (This will take remarkably little time.) Stir gently, especially if you are a slightly nervous cook. Remove the nuts from the oil with a slotted spoon, and spread them on brown paper to cool.

You may want to eat them as soon as they are cool; if not, they may be kept in a tightly covered glass jar for up to 2 weeks.

Makes just over 2 cups.

Zagreb Turtles and Hawley Tortoises

Another pair of neighbors–Jane O'Connor and her husband, chef Philip Keenan–invented this recipe for a chocolate-oriented online service and chat room they used to run called "Coco Cuisine." They designed Zagreb Turtles to highlight an all-natural milk chocolate made in Croatia (hence the name). I used Hershey's, which proved delicious. Feel free to vary the recipe a bit; I tried making half of it with white chocolate and almonds instead of milk chocolate and pecans, and the results were most satisfying. My friend Peter has dubbed that version "Hawley Tortoises."

2 cups sugar
2 cups dark corn syrup
1 cup (2 sticks) sweet butter
2 cups heavy cream
1 pound pecan halves
2 pounds milk chocolate, grated or chopped fine

Directions:

In a large heavy saucepan combine the sugar, the corn syrup, the butter, and 1 cup of the cream. Bring the ingredients to a boil over moderate heat, stirring constantly. Place a candy thermometer into the mixture, and continue boiling and stirring. When the mixture reaches 235 degrees, add the remaining cream, stirring constantly. Allow this mixture to reach 236 degrees on the candy thermometer; then remove it from the heat.

On a large baking sheet (or 2!), greased or lined with parchment paper, dollop the hot caramel a couple of tablespoons at a time. Work each dollop quickly by stirring and stretching it a bit, first with implements and then (when it is cool enough) with your hands. When it is capable of being shaped but still flexible, arrange the pecan halves on top of the caramel. Allow the turtles to cool thoroughly while you melt the chocolate.

Place 2 inches of water in a large, heavy saucepan. Bring the water to a boil and turn off the heat. Place the chopped chocolate in a large stainless-steel bowl on top of the saucepan and stir occasionally as the chocolate melts. Do not allow any water to escape into the chocolate as this will render it useless.

When the turtles are cool and the chocolate is warm, carefully spoon the melted chocolate onto the turtles. Allow them to cool. (This will take several hours.) Store in airtight containers.

Makes 2 to 4 dozen turtles, depending on how big you want to make them. (Mine have ranged from 1-1/2 to 3 inches long.)

Molasses Cookies

Virginia Raymond Taylor is Shirley McMullin's cousin. Ginny obtained this formula from Gertrude Cortis Borden, Ginny's 4-H leader at the Pudding Hollow School 70-odd years ago! These are soft molasses cookies, not snaps, and they bear monitoring in the oven as they burn easily.

1/2 cup shortening
1/2 cup boiling water
1 tablespoon sugar
1 cup molasses
1 teaspoon cider vinegar
1/4 teaspoon ground ginger
1 teaspoon cinnamon
1 pinch salt
3 cups flour
2 teaspoons baking soda
1 egg

Preheat the oven to 400 degrees. Combine the shortening and boiling water. Stir in the sugar, molasses, vinegar, and spices; then add the flour and baking soda. Break the egg into this mixture and blend. Drop small spoonsful of the dough onto greased cookie sheets, and bake for 5 to 6 minutes.

Makes 90 small cookies.

Kate's Fantastic Ginger Snaps

Those who want a bit more snap in their molasses cookie will appreciate this recipe from Kate Stevens of Charlemont. If you're looking for a source for particularly aromatic spices, call the spice merchant Kalustyan's in New York (212-685-3451). Kalustyan's cinnamon in particular is unrivaled, and the store will ship.

3/4 cup (1-1/2 sticks) sweet butter, at room temperature
1 cup sugar plus additional sugar as needed
1 egg
1/4 cup molasses
2 teaspoons baking soda
2 cups flour
1/2 teaspoon salt
1 teaspoon ground cinnamon
1 teaspoon ground ginger
1 teaspoon ground cloves

Preheat the oven to 350 degrees. Cream together the butter and 1 cup sugar, and beat in the egg. Stir in the molasses. In a separate bowl, combine the baking soda, flour, salt, and spices. Combine these dry ingredients with the wet mixture. Roll small balls of the dough (about 3/4 inch in diameter) in granulated sugar, and place them on a greased cookie sheet. Bake for 8 to 10 minutes. Let the cookies stand for a few minutes before removing them from the pan. Makes about 4 dozen cookies.

Pigs in Spring

Learning from Rhubarb

In May and June, my rhubarb patch comes into bloom, lured into renewal by the lengthening days in western Massachusetts. I have always associated rhubarb with New England. Many other regions of the United States either can't grow it or don't appreciate it or both.

When one first encounters it, rhubarb seems bitter and stringy. After closer inspection, one begins to appreciate its deep red color, sober but rich. And one sees that the plant is strong, adaptable, and deep rooted; it clings fiercely to life and to the landscape. A few years ago the McMullins, who live in the heart of Pudding Hollow, tried to raze part of their enormous double rhubarb patch. The condemned stalks defiantly shot up again, more healthy than ever, the following May.

When small and seated at the wooden table in my grandmother's sizeable kitchen in Vermont, I used to turn up my nose at this tart vegetable masquerading as fruit. Now I savor it, not in the least because it reminds me of two strong New England women, one of whom was that very grandmother who force-fed me rhubarb.

Orphaned as a small child, my mother's mother was adopted by a curmudgeonly Vermont bachelor in order to frustrate the many relatives who hoped to inherit his fortune. Her miserly foster father transformed the little girl's life into a pattern we would think a cliche if we encountered it in fiction, part Horatio Alger and part Frances Hodgson Burnett. He fed her on the cheapest possible fare–salt pork and potatoes–and refused to buy her new clothes when this diet made her outgrow her dainty garments. She walked to school in worn-out shoes. In the winter her feet alternately froze from the snow and blistered from the schoolhouse woodstove, too numb to feel their burns until it was too late.

Luckily, by the time she finished grammar school, she found a new home with a kindly neighbor and his wife, a childless couple with plenty of love to spare for a lonely orphan. Once in their care, she flourished, demonstrating a strength nurtured in the literal and figurative winters with her foster father. When she emerged from that period of her life, her colors, like the colors of rhubarb, were deep and true.

The other rhubarb woman of my youth was my neighbor here in Hawley, Mary Parker. The matriarch of a large family, she was called "Gam" by all the children around, as well as by her own grandchildren. A transplant from South Carolina, Gam came to the Massachusetts hills upon her marriage in the early 1920s. She set down deep roots, accustoming herself to northern climes.

Eventually, like rhubarb (another transplant, originating in China), she came to seem more a New Englander than many natives. She rose early and worked a long day, ardently supported the local Congregational church, and both charmed and awed all who knew her. Strict with herself and those around her, she nevertheless cultivated the gifts of love and laughter. Like rhubarb, she was crisp, tart, and tenacious–but receptive to sweetening.

As I begin to harvest and cook my rhubarb patch, I treasure the memories of these two grandmother figures. They taught me to look beyond appearances, to cultivate the patience to deal with stubborn people and fruits, and to retain faith that spring is spreading its rhubarb roots even when the snow is deepest.

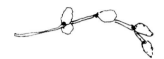

A Note About Harvesting and Preparing Rhubarb

In case you're unfamiliar with rhubarb, here are a few tips for harvesting it.

The most important thing to remember about rhubarb is NOT TO EAT THE LEAVES or even take them into your house. They are poisonous. They are entirely distinct from the stalks, however, so you should have no problem avoiding them.

According to my neighbor Florette, rhubarb should be pulled but never cut. To pick rhubarb, gently pull a stalk in as horizontal a direction as you can manage. (That is, pull it out rather than up from its roots.) It will come right out of the ground. Florette suggests bringing a knife with you when you harvest. After she pulls out her stalks, she immediately cuts off the leaves and the ends of the rhubarb stalks (where they met the ground) and places the leaves and ends back in the rhubarb patch as mulch.

Once you have brought your rhubarb stalks into the house, clean them by letting them soak in cold water in the sink. (You may have to remove a bit of surface dirt later, but this will take care of the worst.) Drain the stalks thoroughly on a towel before using them for cooking. If bits of the rhubarb skin look icky, or if the rhubarb seems very old and tough, you may want to skin your stalks a bit. Otherwise, you are ready to chop and cook.

Stewed Rhubarb

This is the basic dish my grandmother used to serve. The cinnamon is a tradition in our family; if you want more concentrated rhubarb flavor, omit it.

1 pound rhubarb stalks (about 3 cups when cut)
1/2 cup sugar (more if you have a sweet tooth)
1 teaspoon lemon juice
1 teaspoon cinnamon
1/4 cup water

Wash and trim the rhubarb; peel it if it is tough. Cut it into 1-inch pieces. In a heavy saucepan, combine all the ingredients and cover. Cook over low heat for 5 to 7 minutes. Keep an eye on the pot to avoid messy boiling over. Serve plain or add cream or ice cream. Serves 4.

I Got Rhubarb!

This savory dish comes from Michael Collins, the chef and co-owner of the Green Emporium, a glorious neon-decorated restaurant in Colrain. I have become a regular chanteuse at the Emporium, and Mike named this dish in honor of my George Gershwin centenary evening there. He notes that the minor strains of the rhubarb contrast with the major strains of the chicken in true Gershwin fashion. Who could ask for anything more?

4 boneless, skinless chicken breasts
salt and pepper to taste
1/4 teaspoon dried thyme (use a bit more if it's fresh)
extra-virgin olive or canola oil as needed
1 medium onion, chopped
5 stalks rhubarb, chopped
1 cup chicken broth
2 fresh peaches–skinned, pitted, and halved (optional)
more peaches for garnish (optional)

Rub the chicken with the salt, pepper, and thyme. Sauté in the oil until golden. Remove to a warm platter. In the same frying pan, sauté the onion for a few minutes. Then add the rhubarb and broth, and bring to a gentle boil. When the rhubarb softens, remove the mixture from the heat and pop it into a blender. Add the peaches if desired. Blend into a nice puree. Serve this sauce over the chicken, garnishing with additional peaches if you like.

Serves 4.

Rhubarb Bread

This recipe, adapted from one by Hilda Blackmer of Shelburne, dresses up a breakfast or coffee break. Unlike many fruit breads, it is light in color.

1 cup white sugar
2 cups rhubarb stalks, finely chopped
1/4 cup (1/2 stick) melted sweet butter
1 egg, beaten
1/2 cup brown sugar, firmly packed
2 tablespoons grated orange rind
3 cups flour
1/2 teaspoon baking soda
2-1/2 teaspoons baking powder
1/2 teaspoon salt
3/4 cup milk
1-1/2 tablespoons coarse sugar (Florida crystals) or sugar sprinkles

Preheat the oven to 350 degrees. Sprinkle 1/2 cup of the white sugar over the rhubarb and let it stand for 1 to 2 hours. Add the butter, egg, brown sugar, remaining white sugar, and rind to the fruit. Combine the flour, baking soda, baking powder, and salt, and add them to the fruit mixture, alternating with the milk. Place the resulting batter in a greased loaf pan. Sprinkle the coarse sugar on top. Bake for 1 hour.

Makes 1 loaf.

Rhubarb Crisp

This is an adaptation of my grandmother's apple crisp–just about as New Englandy a recipe as you could find. Many people prefer this tart fruit crisp to the apple version. It's delicious by itself or with whipped cream or ice cream.

5 cups rhubarb stalks, cut into 1-inch pieces
1/2 cup white sugar
1/2 cup plus 2 tablespoons flour
1/2 cup regular (not quick) uncooked oatmeal
1 cup brown sugar, firmly packed
1 teaspoon cinnamon
1/4 teaspoon salt
1 stick (1/2 cup) sweet butter, at room temperature

Preheat the oven to 350 degrees. Wash, trim, and chop the rhubarb. Mix the white sugar and 2 tablespoons of the flour and toss in the rhubarb. Spread this mixture in the bottom of a 1-1/2-quart casserole dish, or an 8-by-8-inch pan. Combine the remaining flour, oats, brown sugar, cinnamon, and salt in a bowl. Cut in the butter with two knives until the mixture is crumbly. Spread the butter mixture evenly over the rhubarb. Bake for about 35 minutes, or until the crust is browned. Serves 4 to 6.

Rhubarb Bars

These brownie-like concoctions will convert even recalcitrant children to the love of rhubarb.

3 generous cups chopped rhubarb stalks (about 1-inch pieces)
1-1/2 cups sugar
1 tablespoon lemon juice
1 teaspoon vanilla
2 tablespoons cornstarch, dissolved in 1/4 cup water
1-1/2 cups regular (not quick) uncooked oatmeal
1-1/2 cups flour
1 cup brown sugar, firmly packed
1/2 teaspoon baking soda
1 teaspoon cinnamon
1 cup (2 sticks) sweet butter
1/2 cup chopped nuts (optional)

Preheat the oven to 350 degrees. In a large saucepan, combine the rhubarb, sugar, lemon juice, and vanilla. Add the cornstarch paste and cook over low heat, stirring constantly, until the rhubarb is tender and thick. Set aside to cool. In a medium bowl, mix the dry ingredients and cut the butter into the mixture. Add the nuts, if desired. Pat 3/4 of this crumb mixture into a greased 9-by-13-inch baking dish. Add the cooled rhubarb mixture. Sprinkle the remaining crumbs on top. Bake for 40 minutes.

Makes up to 32 bars, depending on your slicing skills.

Rhubarb Pie

Both my grandmother and Gam loved to bake pies, and rhubarb is never better than in a pie. It tends to juice up even more than most fruits; hence the egg and flour. Strawberries or bits of pineapple make delicious additions to the basic rhubarb pie. An excellent crust for either of the pies on this page may be found on page 147.

1 cup sugar
2 tablespoons flour
a pinch of salt
1 teaspoon cinnamon
1 egg
3 to 4 cups rhubarb pieces, about 1/2-inch long
1 9-inch double pie crust
1 pat sweet butter

Preheat the oven to 425 degrees. In a bowl, mix together the sugar, flour, salt, cinnamon, and egg. Toss in the rhubarb. Put the rhubarb filling into the bottom half of the crust, dot it with the butter, and put on the top. You may use a lattice top; if not, be sure to prick plenty of holes in the top crust. Bake for 10 minutes; then reduce the heat to 350. Bake for 30 to 40 more minutes, until the crust is browned. Serves 6.

Rhubarb Custard Pie

Rhubarb is often called pie plant so here's another pie offering. This recipe comes from the versatile Edward Maeder, who is textile curator at Historic Deerfield. Edward's Swiss-American family taught him to sew and cook at a young age. This pie was a favorite of his grandmother in Wisconsin.

1 unbaked 9-inch pie shell
about 4 cups rhubarb pieces, cut 1/2-inch thick (enough to fill the shell)
3 eggs
1-1/2 cups sugar
1 teaspoon cinnamon
1/4 teaspoon salt
1-1/2 tablespoons flour

Preheat the oven to 425 degrees. Fill the pie shell with the rhubarb pieces. Combine the remaining ingredients, and pour them over the rhubarb. Bake the pie for 10 minutes; then reduce the oven temperature to 350 and cook until the custard is set (when a knife inserted into the pie comes out almost clean). This takes 30 to 50 minutes more, depending upon the juiciness of the rhubarb. Serves 6 to 8.

Florette's Rhubarb Tea

Gam's close friend (and neighbor) Florette came up with this refreshing beverage, which will take care of any excess rhubarb in your garden. (You may make it from frozen rhubarb or frozen rhubarb juice if rhubarb doesn't happen to be in season.)

for the rhubarb juice:
2 pounds rhubarb stalks, chopped (about 6 cups)
3 cups water
1 pinch salt

for the sugar syrup:
2 cups water
3/4 cup sugar

for assembly:
1 quart strong black tea

In a partially covered stainless-steel or enamel saucepan, cook the rhubarb in the water over moderately low heat for 10 to 12 minutes or until tender. Stir gently occasionally to keep from boiling. Cool slightly. Drain the rhubarb in a sieve placed over a bowl and discard the pulp, reserving the liquid. Add the salt.

In another saucepan, combine the ingredients for the sugar syrup. Bring the mixture to a boil, stirring and brushing the sugar crystals from the sides of the pan until the sugar is dissolved. Cook the syrup for 5 minutes, undisturbed, over moderate heat and let it cool.

To make rhubarb tea, combine 2 parts black tea, 1 part rhubarb juice, and 1 part sugar syrup. (You may change these proportions slightly according to your taste.) Serve in a tall glass over ice. As indicated, 4 cups tea, 2 cups rhubarb juice, and 2 cups sugar syrup make 2 quarts of rhubarb tea. Store any leftover juice or syrup in the refrigerator. If you need a double amount of sugar syrup, make 2 separate batches.

Rhubarb Wine

Rachel Kelley of Shelburne makes this wine every year. If you've never made your own wine, do try it—although you may want to quarter the recipe as I did. It's fun, and it tastes a lot more like wine than like rhubarb when you're done.

2 gallons boiling water
2 quarts small pieces of rhubarb stalk
5 pounds sugar
1 pound raisins
1 yeast cake or 1 package dry yeast

Pour the boiling water over the rhubarb. Add the sugar and raisins. Let the mixture cool; then add the yeast. Place the fruit and liquid in a crock. Cover loosely, and let the mixture ferment for 2 weeks, stirring daily. Strain and bottle the wine, loosely capped, until it is settled and clear, several weeks. Then decant it into final bottles and cork tightly.

Makes 3 to 4 quarts.

Rhubarb Fritters

My neighbor Peter Beck came up with this novel way to serve rhubarb for an informal spring dinner party. The tangy rhubarb flavor bursts forth inside the sweet fritter.

2 eggs
1/2 cup sugar
2/3 cup milk
1 teaspoon canola oil
1 teaspoon lemon juice
1 cup flour
1 teaspoon baking powder
1/2 teaspoon salt
1 teaspoon cinnamon
canola oil for frying
2 cups rhubarb pieces, about 1/2-inch each

For the batter: Beat the eggs until they are light. Add the sugar, milk, oil, and lemon juice, and mix well. Combine the dry ingredients, and sift them into the wet mixture. Stir until fairly smooth. (A few lumps will disappear in cooking.) Let the batter sit in the refrigerator for at least an hour.

When ready to fry, pour 2 to 3 inches of oil into a fryer or heavy skillet and heat it to between 350 and 370 degrees. Stab each piece of rhubarb with a fork, and dip it into the batter. Allow it to drip a bit, but don't shake off the batter. Carefully lower the coated rhubarb into the fat, and cook until the first side is brown; then turn and cook the other side. You may cook 5 or 6 pieces at once.

Remove the rhubarb fritters with a slotted spoon, and keep them warm in a 250-degree oven until all are ready. Cover with powdered sugar or warm maple syrup.

Serves 8.

The Kelley Family

An Early Summer Farm & Garden Tour

Franklin Land Trust
Farm and Garden Tour

June 26

The agricultural orientation of rural communities in Massachusetts faces threats from time to time–from natural forces like rocks and weather, and from outside forces like the marketplace and the state legislature.

For two centuries farmers have been battling the rocks that were here long before us, transforming them into stone walls and edges for garden beds. The rocks never seem to go away completely, but their permanence carries with it a certain comfort, even in adversity. Farmers watch and accept the weather. They often find the marketplace and legislature a bit harder to live with.

A number of groups step in and try to defend local agriculture from time to time. One of these is the Franklin Land Trust in Ashfield, which sponsors a tour that is one of my favorite events in Franklin County. It was one of Judy's as well.

At the beginning of each summer, different community members hold a two-day open house for neighbors and visitors, demonstrating the diversity of local uses of landscape, from formal (and informal) gardening to llama farming. Money raised through ticket sales helps the Land Trust preserve the rural character of the area.

In honor of the Land Trust and its efforts, Judy and I planned this chapter as a culinary survey of some of our favorite farms and gardens. A few have been featured on the tour. Others never will be but join the regulars in making careful and loving use of the land in the hills about them.

Rachel Kelley's Dandelion Wine

Rachel Kelley is a delightful senior citizen. She and her late husband Ernest farmed all their lives in Shelburne on a small homestead. Ernie was a true Yankee character in a tersely humorous, uniquely New England way; he told wonderful stories of past farming days. Rachel dresses in ruffles and prints, sporting gently curled hair and a cheery smile. The Kelleys work hard and eat well. Like their rural forefathers, they still reserve different days of the week for different projects, and Rachel has a regular baking day in which she produces the pies and cakes that have made her reputation around the county. Here I reproduce her recipe for a family favorite, dandelion wine. Rachel recommends collecting the dandelion blossoms after a spring shower so that they will be free of dust. She also suggests snipping the yellow petals off the caps with a pair of old scissors; she finds the green caps a bit bitter. A note: I found when working on this wine that it takes a LONG time to pick dandelion petals, so I quartered the recipe. You might like to do the same—or to enlist stalwart helpers.

8 quarts boiling water
4 quarts dandelion petals
4 large oranges, cut into small slices
2 lemons, cut into small slices
5 pounds sugar
1 pound raisins
1 pound currants (optional)
1/2 yeast cake or 1 teaspoon dry yeast

Bring the water to a boil, and add the petals. Boil for 5 minutes, stirring. Let the liquid stand overnight in a nonmetallic container; then strain through several layers of cheesecloth. (Don't squeeze!) Add the remaining ingredients; if using dry yeast, dissolve it in a small amount of water before adding. Let the mixture stand for 2 weeks in a loosely covered crock, stirring daily; then strain and store it in loosely capped jars until the top liquid is clear and the sediment has settled, a few weeks at least. Decant the wine into bottles, and cork or cap them tightly. Makes about 1-1/2 gallons.

Harvard Beets

This recipe comes from Ethel White, my neighbor who farms, gardens, keeps house, and serves as the hostess for the library bookmobile when it comes to Hawley every other month. Ethel is as proud of her cooking as she is of the gorgeous flowers that border her house in summer; she grows model roses, gloriosa daisies, and sunflowers. For most of her life she has baked a pie every single day for her husband Bob's lunch. This sweet-and-sour concoction makes use of a vegetable that bursts with color, the beet.

2 cups cooked or canned beets
1/2 cup sugar
1/2 tablespoon cornstarch
1/4 cup vinegar
1/4 cup water
1/2 teaspoon salt
2 tablespoons sweet butter

Slice the beets (unless you are using baby beets, in which case they are attractive and delicious whole). Mix together the sugar and cornstarch in a saucepan. Add the vinegar, water, and salt. Mix this combination well, and boil it for 5 minutes. Add the beets, and simmer for 30 minutes. Just before serving, bring the liquid to the boiling point, and stir in the butter. Serves 6.

Aunt Lizzie's Ginger Drink

This recipe comes from a farm in Virginia Raymond Taylor's memory. A native of Hawley, she now lives in Charlemont. "I remember taking this to the fields on a hot summer day for the men to drink while they were taking a breather from haying," she says. The formula for this tangy beverage came to her from her great-aunt, Elizabeth Atkins of Hawley, through Elizabeth's sister-in-law (and Virginia's grandmother) Carrie Atkins Gould. I make a small quantity of it from time to time with soda water for my small nephew Michael, who likes it better than store-bought ginger ale.

1 heaping teaspoon ground ginger
1/2 cup sugar
2 quarts cold water
1 cup maple syrup
1/2 cup vinegar

Mix the ginger and the sugar together with a bit of the water, then combine this mixture with the rest of the ingredients. Stir until dissolved.

Makes just over 2 quarts.

Pine Brook Farm

Pine Brook Farm Dill Bread

Although their beautiful farmhouse in Buckland was built in 1810, Polly and Dave Bartlett didn't own it until 1967. At that time it hadn't been lived in year round for years and suffered from major neglect. "Everything that had not broken took the first month to break," Polly remembers. "Everything you touched was ready to give up." The pair and their children had to use camping equipment to get through the first few weeks, which unfortunately fell in December. The furnace hadn't been used for years, and the Bartletts found themselves stuffing rags under every door in order to keep even remotely warm. Little by little, they have brought life back to the place. It is now a cozy home that reflects its age but also the love expended on it. The Bartletts have horses they love and keep a large garden with beehives. Their gardening arrangement takes advantage of their differing skills: Dave grows, and Polly picks. Polly then makes delicious concoctions from the garden products and honey. She makes this bread with garden-fresh dill.

2 cups creamed cottage cheese
2 tablespoons sweet butter
2 tablespoons plus fresh dill weed
(or half as much dried)
2 tablespoons minced scallion
1/4 cup sugar
1/4 teaspoon baking soda
2 teaspoons salt
2 eggs, beaten
1/2 cup lukewarm water
1 package active dry yeast
5 to 6 cups unbleached flour

Warm the cottage cheese and butter. Add the dill, scallions, sugar, baking soda, salt, and eggs. Beat until blended.

Combine the water and yeast. When the yeast has dissolved, stir it and the water into the cottage-cheese mixture. Stir in as much flour as possible, and knead in more until the dough is no longer sticky.

Place the dough in a greased bowl. Cover and let it rise until it doubles in bulk. Punch down the dough, and shape it into 2 loaves. Let it rise again until doubled.

Bake in greased loaf pans in a preheated 375-degree oven for 35 to 45 minutes.

Makes 2 loaves.

Pat's Risotto Primavera

Pat Leuchtman, a horticultural writer and librarian, lives high on a hill in Heath at the end of a dirt road. Working with love and a great pile of manure, she manages to produce a symphony of roses each year–wild roses and English roses, shrub roses and heritage roses–just in time for her annual rose-viewing party at the end of June. A special group of roses came from local farm wives. Pat calls them her Farmgirls and has named them after their donors: Rachel, Terri, Susan, and Fred. Pat doesn't actually cook anything with the roses; they are purely decorative. She did present me with this garden-oriented risotto recipe, however. Her quantities for the vegetables (and indeed the types of vegetables listed) are only intended as a suggestion; she often doubles the amounts of the vegetables, and she tends to throw in whatever she has in the garden instead of sticking to the recipe. Believe it or not, she has already cut down on the butter from her original recipe; you may cut it down more if you desire.

1/2 cup (1 stick) sweet butter
2/3 cup chopped onion
1-1/4 cups Arborio or long-grain rice
3/4 cup white wine
1/4 cup green beans, diced
1/4 cup thinly sliced carrots
1/4 cup zucchini in small slices
3 cups simmering chicken stock
2 tablespoons diced fresh tomatoes
4 teaspoons chopped parsley
1/2 cup grated Parmesan cheese

Melt half of the butter and add the onion. Cook, stirring, for 5 minutes. Add the rice. Cook for 1 minute. Add 1/2 cup of the wine plus the vegetables, and stir. Add 1 cup of stock and keep stirring. As the mixture cooks and dries up, add the remaining stock a bit at a time. Cooking will take quite a while–somewhere between half an hour and 45 minutes. (In my experience, the only sure-fire way to know whether risotto is done is to taste it.) Just before serving, add the tomatoes, the parsley, the remaining wine and butter, and the cheese. Serves 6.

Pesto Butter for Sweet Corn

Corn isn't generally in season yet when the Land Trust has its Farm and Garden Tour, but this recipe is so simple and so summer fresh that I had to include it. It comes from Nikki Ciesluk of Ciesluk Farm in South Deerfield. The farm stand is a bit far from Pudding Hollow, but Nikki grew up in the West County town of Buckland so there's undoubtedly a bit of local tang in this garlicky spread!

1 cup fresh basil leaves
1/2 cup freshly grated Parmesan cheese
2 tablespoons crushed garlic
1/2 cup (1 stick) sweet butter, quartered

In a food processor, finely chop the basil leaves. Add the Parmesan cheese and garlic, and mix. Add the pieces of butter to the food processor, and process the mixture until finely blended. Transfer the pesto butter into a small crock. Chill it in the refrigerator for at least a half hour. Makes enough butter for 13 ears of corn.

Elsa Bakalar's Garden-Party Trifle

English-born Elsa Bakalar often serves this delicious trifle at garden parties. Elsa and her garden are celebrities in West County and elsewhere; she tours extensively, talking to garden clubs and selling her gorgeous book, A Garden of One's Own. *In her conversation, as in her book, Elsa is both engaging and inspirational. "In the garden," she says with a smile, "you do what pleases you. There are very few areas, it seems to me, in which we have a sense of being in control. Much of our life is out of control rather badly. And in the garden—it's a fallacy, of course, but you have the feeling that you're in control. I mean, there's always some dandelion that puts you in your place. But it's calming, by and large. It's simply beautiful. We could all do with more beauty." Of this trifle Elsa says, "This is the ultimate show-off dessert for parties. It looks wonderful, tastes even better, and adds to the festivities!" She uses a footed glass bowl to show off her creation. I didn't have one, so I used a casserole dish when testing the recipe; the dish still tasted luxurious.*

for the base:
lady fingers (18 to 24, depending on the shape of your serving dish)
1 cup raspberry jam
1/2 cup almonds, slivered and halved
3/4 cup sweet sherry

for the custard:
1-1/2 cups milk
1 cup heavy cream
4 tablespoons sugar
5 eggs, well beaten
1 teaspoon cornstarch
(optional: for "the faint of heart" who might worry about the custard's ability to set firmly, says Elsa)
1 teaspoon vanilla

for the topping:
2 cups whipped cream
fresh raspberries, shaved chocolate, or toasted almonds

Split the lady fingers and spread them with half of the jam. Sprinkle them with the almonds. Arrange them on the bottom and sides of your bowl, split sides facing in. Drip the sherry on the lady fingers and allow it to soak in while you make the English cream custard.

Heat the milk and cream in the top of a double boiler until warm to the touch. Add the sugar to the eggs—and the cornstarch, if desired. Pour the heated milk and cream onto the egg mixture, and return the liquid to the double boiler. Stir it over low heat until it is thick but not boiling. Add the vanilla. Pour the custard into the bowl, and let it cool slightly; then place it in the refrigerator. Leave it there until it is firm, at least 2 hours.

When the custard has set, add another thin layer of raspberry jam, and cover the whole with the whipped cream. Decorate according to your taste, with shaved dark chocolate, toasted almonds, or—best of all—fresh raspberries from the garden, added immediately before serving. Serves 8 elegantly.

Goat Cheese à la Blue Heron Farm

Bill and Norma Coli are city dwellers who found their dream, and their dream house (dating back to the 1700s), in Charlemont several years ago and haven't looked back since. Blue Heron Farm serves as a working farm as well as a guest house. The Colis raise two major types of working animals. Their Norwegian Fjord horses decorate the landscape with their sturdy blond bodies; they also tow the Colis' cart around the farm and around town. Their goats provide milk to sell as well as a lot of work for Norma. Still just a bit cosmopolitan in style, she looks glamorous even as she mucks out the barn in her work jeans. The dairy thermometer needed to make the cheese (as well as many other cheesemaking goodies) may be purchased from New England Cheesemaking Supply in the West County town of Ashfield (413-628-3808). You may have to call around a bit to find fresh goat milk; ask your local health-food store or state agricultural agency for suggestions.

1 quart fresh goat milk
(not more than 48 hours old)
2 tablespoons dill-garlic-peppercorn vinegar
(or another herbal vinegar–see page 126)
salt, pepper, and dill, to taste

Directions:

Heat the milk in a double boiler (the top half should be non-aluminum) until it reaches 180 degrees on a dairy thermometer. Cook the milk for another 10 minutes, monitoring it constantly and adjusting the heat to keep it as close to 180 degrees as you can.

When your 10 minutes are up, remove the top pan from the double boiler, and stir the vinegar into the milk using a sterilized, stainless-steel slotted spoon. (Just stir until mixed; don't overdo it.) Set the pan aside for 20 to 30 minutes to allow the milk to curdle; then ladle the fresh curds into a colander lined with cheesecloth.

Allow the curds to drain for 4 to 6 hours, or until the cheese looks like cheese. You may want to scrape your cheesecloth from time to time to help the curds drain. You may also tie the cheesecloth into a knot and suspend it above a bowl to assist with drainage. (Be careful not to spill your curds if you do this; you can go through an awful lot of cheesecloth this way.)

Place the cheese in a bowl, and add salt and pepper to taste. It's fun to shape your cheese into a log and roll the log in dill. (Fresh is best, but good dried dill weed will do.) You'll have about 2/3 of a cup of cheese, which will last in the refrigerator for a week.

Round Garden Pasta Salad

The glamorous Florette shook up our neighborhood by designing a circular garden outside her barn-inspired home, which she named Hawleywood. She created this versatile salad to show off one of the area's most delectable early fresh vegetables, asparagus. If asparagus is not in season, any other fresh vegetable will do–parboiled snap peas or string beans, raw zucchini or broccoli. The salad may be doubled or tripled to feed a large party or cut down for a cozy dinner for two.

for the salad:
1 pound bow-tie pasta
(or the shape of your choice)
2 cups fresh asparagus cut in 1-inch pieces, boiled for about 2 minutes then drained and cooled with ice cubes
1 red bell pepper, cut into small pieces
30 Greek olives, pitted and halved
1 cup crumbled feta cheese

for the dressing:
4 tablespoons red wine vinegar
1 splash of water
1 garlic clove, minced
1/2 teaspoon salt
1 teaspoon sugar
3 tablespoons chopped fresh parsley, plus 1 tablespoon for garnish
1/2 teaspoon dried or 1 teaspoon fresh oregano or basil
ground pepper
10 tablespoons extra-virgin olive oil

Cook the pasta according to the directions on the package, making sure that it is not too well done; al dente is preferred. While the pasta is boiling, you may cook the asparagus, cut up the red pepper, and assemble the ingredients for the dressing in a jar.

When the pasta has drained and cooled slightly, combine it in a large bowl with the asparagus and pepper pieces. Shake the dressing and pour about half onto the salad, mixing well. Chill the mixture for a couple of hours. Taste it to see how flavorful and moist it is; chances are you will want to add more dressing at this point. (If you don't use all of the dressing, don't worry; it's delicious on a green salad.)

Toss in the olives and feta cheese and mix thoroughly. Chill again for an hour or two, stir once more, throw a bit more chopped parsley over all, and serve.

Serves 10 to 12.

A Mustard Sauce Inspired by Mary Dole

Mary Dole arrived in Shelburne in 1941 as a bride. "I remember very distinctly," she recalls, "a couple coming over to visit me. She said, 'Now you have come to Shelburne, and you may spend the rest of your life in Shelburne, but you won't be a native.'" The Dole family received the first deeds to their extensive property in colonial times, although the house in which Mary lives was built only in 1858 by her late husband's grandfather. When Mary moved in, the house had no electricity (it was electrified during World War II), and she used a wood stove to heat all her meals. She still prefers her meat cooked with wood. Mary Dole's house is a tangible link with the past. Her kitchen includes much of its original equipment, plus an enormous long pantry. Strolling through the farmhouse, one spots old and new family treasures. The high point of the tour may be the living room, which features trophies for the Doles' illustrious line of milking short-horn cattle. The family owns one of the oldest continuing herds in the country. Large oil paintings of these stately beasts vie for attention with the many ribbons they have won at fairs—and with the room's gorgeous fading fleur-de-lis wallpaper, which dates from the house's construction. Coming out of the house to gaze at the husky cattle on Mary Dole's hills, one appreciates her herding and housekeeping traditions. After all these years, she has finally become a native. Judy and I spent months trying to cajole a recipe out of Mary Dole with absolutely no luck; either modesty or lack of interest in cooking made her say she had nothing special to share. So I include a non-Dole beef accompaniment to pay tribute to Mary and her cows. This mustard sauce comes from my neighbors Susan and Peter Purdy. It makes an excellent accompaniment to roast beef or pot roast (or even ham).

1 egg yolk 1/2 pint light cream 1-1/2 tablespoons dry mustard 1 rounded tablespoon flour 1/2 cup sugar 1/4 teaspoon salt 1/2 cup cider vinegar	Beat the egg yolk in a saucepan. Add the cream. Sift together the dry ingredients, and add them to the egg mixture. Cook until thick, stirring constantly. At the same time, heat the vinegar separately. When the yolk mixture is ready, remove both pans from the heat and add the vinegar to the rest of the sauce. Makes just under 2 cups.

When This Old Hat Was New

Ernie Kelley loved to recite this poem while wearing a hat in which his grandfather saw service in the Civil War. In fact, both his grandfather and the hat were shot–seriously, but not fatally. The bullet, Ernie explained, "went right through the brim, took out the eye, and went through the other side of his head." Since Ernie's death his nephew Fred has taken over the tradition of sharing the poem with members of the Sons and Daughters of Hawley at their August annual meeting.

When this old hat was new
The railroad was a stage,
And the six-mule team made plenty of steam
On a moderate kind of a gauge.
When we needed a pen, we got a quill from a goose.
The ink we used was blue.
And the women we loved didn't want to be men
When this old hat was new.

At Mary Dole's

Mindy's Cat and My Window in June

Bountiful Berries

Summer's greatest joy to New Englanders is probably the season's almost excessive sunshine–the golden days that dawn before we waken and endure through most of our evening activities, making up with gusto for winter's abbreviated hours of light.

Our second greatest sensual treat stems from that sunshine. It consists of the foods of summer, the fruits and vegetables that we cannot obtain fresh at any other time of year.

Everyone has a favorite summer food. One friend of mine concentrates on tomatoes, consuming their ripe, red flesh daily from the garden as long as they last. Another plumps for corn; a third, for peaches. (Perhaps predictably, nobody I know lists zucchini as a favorite summer food, although everyone I know eats it with grudging appreciation of its versatility–not to mention its unstoppability!)

My favorite summer produce is in fact a series of crops. I glory in New England's berries. A simple gift of nature, appreciated for centuries, berries are easy to come by; I can pick them wild or purchase them fresh nearby. As they ripen in turn, these fruits reflect and reinforce the rhythms of my summer.

Fat, juicy strawberries mark the youthful onset of the season. They thrive in New England's long days of summer; California products simply can't compete. Kneeling and nibbling in a sun-bloated patch as I gather them, I always end up with a pink nose, pink clothing, and a delightful gorged feeling. I've never learned to pick strawberries neatly, and I'm not sure I want to. Excess is what they're all about.

The more restrained raspberry follows the strawberry as July follows June. I have had limited success in growing raspberries, but I can always find a few wild in nearby fields or purchase them fresh from a more conscientious cultivator. Their delicate, aristocratic flavor tempts the palate as the sun grows hotter. And their price commands a healthy respect for the value of luxury fruits.

Early August brings blueberries into markets and bowls. Like summer in August, blueberries are mature and perhaps just a bit staid but evoke appreciation nevertheless. My blueberry of choice is the tiny variety that grows profusely on the hills of Heath. The ideal growing conditions in this hilltown include a high elevation and the sort of rocky soil that inspired old-time New Englanders to construct their boundary walls of stone.

Heathens (that is, residents of Heath) shepherd their produce along by praying for rain and by doing their best to repel the bears, birds, and deer that share humans' love of berries. Some of the growers also indulge in an old Native American cultivating trick: they carefully burn a section of their blueberry patch each year, ensuring a richer crop the following season. The tasty products of these endeavors are small in many ways. Their bushes grow low to the ground, and their fruit is tiny by conventional standards.

The flavor of the berries, however, is big–sweet and concentrated. They don't get squishy like fat, cultivated blueberries. Moreover, they preserve like a dream, filling my freezer with small pearls I can use year-round for baking or just pop onto my morning cereal.

The final berry in my summer and my environs is the blackberry, the companion of late August evenings in which sweaters and shawls begin to make their appearance. My blackberry-picking journey takes me each year to a profuse patch on the other side of town. Adjacent to a now defunct church, it provided berry suppers to an active congregation decades ago. Now it attracts only enough pickers to make clear paths through its richness–and to share the secret with a select few. Made into pies or tossed directly into the mouth, the berries carry a slight tartness that reminds me of those past pickers and conveys a hint of the autumn to come.

Here I offer a favorite recipe or two for each of these berries. Don't forget to savor them by themselves, however, and let their differing flavors and textures underline and enhance the progress of summer.

Strawberry Cake

This member of the pound-cake family tastes lusciously of butter and berries. The recipe was adapted from one distributed by one of the many pick-your-own patches in Franklin County, Nourse Farms. Feel free to add many more strawberries than the recipe calls for; I always do. One warning: Do not overbeat this cake, or it will become crumbly.

1 cup (2 sticks) sweet butter, at room temperature
1-1/2 cups sugar
4 eggs
2 tablespoons vanilla
3 cups flour
1 tablespoon baking powder
1-1/2 teaspoons salt
2/3 cup milk
1 cup chopped, fresh strawberries
confectioner's sugar (optional)

Preheat the oven to 350 degrees. Cream the butter until light; then add the sugar and mix well. Beat in the eggs, 1 at a time, and add the vanilla. Combine the dry ingredients and add them to the batter alternately with the milk. Fold in the berries. Bake in a greased 10-inch bundt pan for about 1 hour, or until a toothpick inserted into the cake comes out clean.

Cool the cake in its pan for 25 minutes; then remove it and sprinkle it with confectioner's sugar if you want extra sweetness and a bit of decor. Serves 10 to 12.

Strawberry-Rhubarb Jam

You may of course make plain strawberry jam, but I love to include the rhubarb; it adds flavor, texture, and pectin to the proceedings. Don't try to double this recipe, or you'll have to cook the jam forever.

2 cups strawberries
2 cups rhubarb pieces (stalks only)
1 tablespoon lemon juice
3 cups sugar
1 pat (about 1 teaspoon) sweet butter (to prevent foaming)

Cook the fruit and lemon juice over low heat until tender. (You may or may not have to add a tiny bit of water to keep the fruit from burning at first.) Add the sugar and butter, and cook rapidly until thick, stirring frequently. The jam is ready when it sheets off a cold, stainless-steel spoon. Remove any foam you see (there shouldn't be too much, thanks to the butter). Stir the jam for 5 minutes before you ladle it into sterilized jars; this keeps the fruit from rising to the top of the jars when cooled. Process in a boiling-water bath for 5 minutes. (See "About Processing," page 123.) Makes about 4 cups.

Raspberries with Chocolate Chantilly

Chantilly is, of course, whipped cream. My neighbor Florette first introduced me to this easy but elegant dish, designed to appeal to those who like the delicate blend of chocolate and raspberry. If you want to make it even easier, don't bother folding the raspberries into the chocolate cream; just arrange them artistically in large dollops of the whipped-cream mixture.

1 cup heavy cream
1/4 cup sugar
4 teaspoons cocoa
1/2 teaspoon vanilla
1 pint fresh raspberries

In a mixing bowl using an electric mixer, beat the cream, slowly adding the sugar and cocoa. When the cream is almost stiff, add the vanilla, and turn off the mixer before you end up with chocolate butter! Gently fold the raspberries into the chocolate cream, and serve immediately. Serves 4.

Raspberry Cordial

This recipe from Joanne McMullin preserves the flavor of fresh raspberries as no jam could. The resulting cordial may be drunk by itself, served on fruit salad, or combined with homemade peach preserves on ice cream to make a variant of peach melba.

4 cups fresh raspberries
1 cup sugar
vodka as needed

Place the berries in a 1-quart mason jar. Pour the sugar in over them. Then fill the jar with vodka, cover it, and place it in a cool, dark place. Gently shake and/or turn the bottle twice daily until the sugar dissolves. At the end of 6 weeks, strain out your cordial. (The perfectly preserved if boozy berries should at this point be added to a fruit salad or punch; don't waste them!) This recipe makes 2 cups, more or less, depending on the juiciness of your berries.

Blueberry Muffins

Jack Cable, one of Heath's major berry farmers, offers a prize every year at the Heath Fair for the best blueberry recipe. This recipe, from The Heath Fair Cookbook, *comes from his family.*

2 eggs, separated
1 cup sugar
1/2 cup (1 stick) sweet butter at room temperature
1/4 teaspoon salt
1 teaspoon vanilla
1-1/2 cups flour
1 teaspoon baking powder
1/3 cup milk
1-1/2 cups blueberries
sugar for sprinkling (colored sugar is fun)
cupcake or muffin liners as needed

Preheat the oven to 350 degrees. Beat the egg whites until stiff. Add 1/4 cup sugar slowly while beating. In another bowl, cream the butter. Add to it the salt, vanilla, remaining sugar, and egg yolks. Combine the flour and the baking powder and add them to the main batter alternately with the milk. Fold in the blueberries, followed by the egg whites. Place the batter in lined muffin tins, and sprinkle the muffin tops with sugar. Bake for 20 to 30 minutes. Makes about 18 muffins.

Blueberry Butter

I've never been completely happy with blueberry jam, which often cooks up too sweet. I enjoy this butter, however, which combines blueberry flavor with apple butter. It may be spread on toast or added to yogurt.

4 cups apple puree
(created by cooking apples in a saucepan with a small amount of water, then straining them through a food mill)
5 cups blueberries, fresh or frozen
3 cups white sugar
1-1/2 cups brown sugar, firmly packed
1-1/2 teaspoons cinnamon
1/2 teaspoon allspice
1/2 teaspoon nutmeg (generous)
1 teaspoon lemon juice
1 dab sweet butter

Place all the ingredients in a large saucepan, and cook over low heat until the sugars dissolve, stirring constantly. Increase the heat and bring the mixture to a boil; then lower the heat and simmer until the butter thickens (45 minutes to 1 hour), stirring frequently–especially toward the end.

Pour the butter into sterilized jars, cover and seal, and process in a boiling water bath for 10 minutes. (See "About Processing," page 123.)

Makes 6 to 7 cups.

Blueberry Crisp

This is a basic fruit crisp. Eat it with whipped cream or ice cream–or just by itself, warm and slightly crunchy.

6 cups blueberries
4 tablespoons tapioca
1 tablespoon lemon juice
1 cup regular (not quick) uncooked oatmeal
1/2 cup flour, scant
1-1/2 teaspoons cinnamon
1/2 teaspoon salt
2/3 cup brown sugar, firmly packed
1/3 cup white sugar
3/4 cup (1-1/2 sticks) sweet butter

Preheat the oven to 350 degrees. Combine the berries, tapioca, and lemon juice in a large casserole dish. Allow them to sit for 10 to 15 minutes. In a separate bowl, combine the remaining dry ingredients, and cut the butter into them until the mixture is crumbly. Smooth it on top of the berry mixture, covering it completely. Bake for 35 to 45 minutes–or a bit longer if your berries are very juicy.

Serves 8.

Blackberry Sally Lunn

This simple coffee cake comes from my mother Jan, a basic but wonderful cook. It may be made with almost any kind of berry, but it thrives on tart blackberries.

1/2 cup (1 stick) sweet butter at room temperature
1/2 cup white sugar
2 eggs
1-3/4 cups flour
1 tablespoon baking powder
1/2 teaspoon salt
1 cup milk
1 to 1-1/2 cups blackberries
1/3 cup brown sugar, firmly packed
1/3 teaspoon cinnamon

Preheat the oven to 350 degrees. Cream together the butter and white sugar. Beat the eggs together and then beat them into the butter-sugar combination. Sift together the flour, baking powder, and salt; then add those dry ingredients and the milk, alternately, to the butter-sugar-egg mixture. Fold in the berries.

Pour the batter into a greased 8-by-8-inch baking dish, and top with the brown sugar and cinnamon. Bake for 50 minutes. Serves 9 (with big pieces) to 16 (with tiny pieces).

Blackberry Pudding

This relatively low-fat dessert (until you pile something creamy on top of it!) is adapted from a recipe by former summer resident Toni Leitner. It resembles an upside-down cake.

2 cups blackberries
the juice of 1/2 lemon
1/2 teaspoon cinnamon
1-3/4 cups sugar
3 tablespoons sweet butter at room temperature
1/2 cup milk
1 cup flour
1 teaspoon baking powder
1/4 teaspoon salt plus a dash
1 tablespoon cornstarch
1 cup boiling water

Preheat the oven to 375 degrees. Combine the blackberries, lemon juice, and cinnamon, and spread the mixture into a well greased, 8-inch-square pan.

Cream 3/4 cup sugar with the butter and add the milk. Sift together the flour, the baking powder, and 1/4 teaspoon salt, and add them to the butter mixture. Spread that batter over the berries. Mix together the remaining sugar and salt with the cornstarch, and sprinkle them over the batter. Pour the water over the top, but do not stir it in.

Bake for 1 hour. Serve hot. This pudding forms a sauce so it may be served with or without whipped cream or ice cream. Serves 9.

Shelburne Falls Coffee Roasters' Mixed-Berry Scones

Finally, here's a recipe in which you may use any type of berry you choose—or mix a couple of berry types. Each day the Shelburne Falls Coffee Roasters sell dozens of these pastries to accompany the coffee roasted and sold by the couple who head the enterprise, Curtis Rich and Kathy Lytle. I have adapted the recipe slightly. (The Coffee Roasters routinely make 6 times this much batter!) The scones tend to spread on the pan. If you want to look ahead from berry season to the fall, try substituting chopped apple pieces for the berries, and top the scones with cinnamon sugar.

1/2 cup sugar
2 cups flour
1-1/2 teaspoons baking powder
1 teaspoon baking soda
1/2 teaspoon salt
6 tablespoons (3/4 stick) sweet butter
2/3 cup fresh mixed berries (dried berries, raisins, or dried cranberries also work well)
1 egg
2/3 cup buttermilk
1/2 teaspoon vanilla
additional sugar as needed (optional)

Preheat the oven to 325 degrees. Combine the sugar, flour, baking powder, baking soda, and salt. Cut in the butter, but be careful not to overmix. Stir the berries into this mixture.

In a separate bowl, combine the egg, buttermilk, and vanilla. Add the berry mixture and blend briefly. Place the dough on a floured surface, and knead it a few times with well floured hands. Cut the dough into 6 to 8 pieces, and place them on a greased baking sheet. Sprinkle sugar on top if desired for added flavor and crunch. Bake for 18 to 25 minutes. Makes 6 to 8 scones.

The Playhouse

Playhouse Parties
Making Food & Making Music

Many of our neighbors in the hilltowns do not live in the area full time. Since the early days of the 20th century, our comforting hills and lullabying brooks have attracted city dwellers who join us for the summer. They show up on Memorial Day weekend, signaling the arrival of the busiest season. They stay through the strawberry days of June, the mosquito nights of July, and the golden hours of August, leaving on Labor Day but usually making a brief return journey to view the brilliant color of Columbus Day weekend.

The recipes that follow all come from the residents of the summer community in which I grew up, Singing Brook Farm in Hawley. The Farm, as we call it, was among Hawley's first summer residences. In 1919 Gordon Parker, a young businessman from eastern Massachusetts, bought a farm in Hawley from Amelia Sears. The only remaining member of her family, Miss Sears was happy to leave her rocky homestead to move in with friends down the road. Much to Gordon Parker's surprise, she left him the farm animals as well as the house, the furniture, the meadows, the trees, and the brook that gave his new property its name.

Gordon found a hired hand to keep an eye on the animals while he was back east. He then made himself at home on his new property, inviting a succession of young women to visit Singing Brook Farm. He promptly married the one who suited it (and him) best, a young southerner named Mary Stuart. He chose an extraordinary woman—strong, intelligent, and indefatigable. She bore and raised five children, helped him with his business (running it after his death), and happily settled in Hawley temporarily every summer and permanently upon her retirement from full-time work.

The Parkers bought land adjacent to their original farm as it became available and erected a number of structures on their property. They started by building summer cabins for their children, later expanding to erect more small houses for summer rental. As the Parker children grew to adulthood and started having children of their own, the then-widowed Mary (the "Gam" of my rhubarb chapter) sought out renters who would have something in common with her children and grandchildren. The renters included my parents.

Most of these summer tenants fell into one of two camps, corresponding to the interests of young Alice Parker, a composer, or her brother Harrison (Harry), who worked on rural development in India and Indonesia. So I grew up surrounded by musicians and people who traveled frequently to Asia–an odd mixture, but one that worked surprisingly well.

us children appropriately glamorous crops, from Jerusalem artichokes to the tallest sunflowers we had ever seen. And most of us had a patch of something growing near our cabins–tomatoes, basil, berries, or at least (in the case of my family, pretty hopeless gardeners) a few sprigs of mint for iced tea.

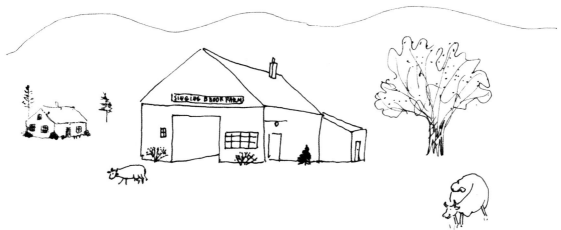

Singing Brook Farm in the summertime resembled a camp for adults and children alike. By chance or by Mary Parker's careful choice, most of the residents and renters turned out to be enthusiastic cooks and gardeners. Gam herself had a huge garden in which we were all encouraged to work. (She scrupulously adhered to her motto: "Them as weeds, eats.") The fascinating Florette Zuelke, a talented New Yorker who worked at Columbia Records and had attended Juilliard with Alice, grew a variety of what seemed to

We played and watched tennis; swam in the Dam, our frigid but clear dammed-up stream; and gathered for exciting evening parties in the Playhouse, a spacious rectangular structure behind the old Sears farmhouse. Originally used by the Parkers as a recreation area for their children, by the time those children grew up the Playhouse was primarily a place for parties. Decorated with lanterns and puppets from Harrison's travels to Indonesia, it was a festive, magical space. Potluck Playhouse parties, held on special weekends during the summer, drew the members of our small community together to eat, drink, and entertain each other.

In the afternoon before each party, Farm children were conscripted by Gam to sweep the Playhouse; arrange the wicker furniture; and make sure that silverware and paper-plate holders were clean and in place. We hurried home to change, then returned with our parents and a plethora of aromatic dishes. After an extended cocktail hour (after all, no one had to drive anywhere after dinner!), we applied ourselves to the business of eating and awaited the evening's entertainment. We were never disappointed. Recitations were particularly popular. After two bourbons, my mother Jan was easily persuaded to narrate "The Owl and the Pussycat." Gam and Aunt Hel Gibbons (a spry contemporary of the senior Parkers) would rummage through a dress-up trunk and don costumes to enact the title characters, and my mother would chronicle their adventures dramatically. Sometimes adults or children recited humorous poems of our own devising; Gam offered prizes. My father Abe told wonderful stories that rewrote history in ingenious fashion. And we made lots of music.

Alice's husband Tom Pyle, a professional baritone, could move us to tears with his voice. By evening's end we were all joining in, singing hymns, spirituals, folk songs, and American popular standards from "L'il Liza Jane" to "Stardust." Talent was less important than enthusiasm.

Vacation patterns have changed, and Singing Brook Farm is quieter than it was when I was growing up. Gam died in 1989, and renters come for weeks rather than for months or for the whole summer. Even so, Parkers, renters, and neighbors still gather once or twice a summer in the Playhouse–and for a few hours we recapture the spirit of a Singing Brook Farm in which making food and making music were a way of life.

Uncle Abe's Orange and Onion Salad

My father Abe was not exactly a whiz in the kitchen. Nevertheless, he always enjoyed preparing this simple yet elegant salad for his friends at Singing Brook Farm. (It's even simpler if you get someone else to wash the lettuce and slice the oranges and onions for you as he did!)

lettuce as needed for a bed
3 oranges, peeled, then sliced and seeded
a dash of sugar
1/2 red onion, sliced
salt and pepper to taste
1 tablespoon extra virgin olive oil
1 teaspoon red wine vinegar

Line a salad bowl with the lettuce. On top, line alternating layers of the orange slices, sugar, red onion, and salt and pepper. Combine the oil and vinegar and drizzle them over the salad. Look impressive while dishing it up.

Serves 8.

Esty's Secret Smoked Lox

This recipe comes from a Singing Brook Farm visitor named Esty Epstein, a lively Frenchwoman who often comes to stay with summer renter Bobbie Carlin. The hardest thing about it is locating the liquid smoke in a grocery store. The first time I made this dish, I cut the recipe in half, figuring I wouldn't be able to use 2 whole pounds of faux smoked salmon. My single pound went so fast, however, that I have made the full recipe ever since.

8 teaspoons Kosher salt
3 tablespoons sugar
2 tablespoons liquid smoke
2 pounds salmon fillet

Mix the first three ingredients together, and spread them over the salmon. Wrap the salmon tightly in plastic wrap; then place it in a plastic bag and seal. Place the bag in a baking dish, and weigh the salmon down with bricks or cans. Refrigerate for 8 days, turning it daily.

When the salmon has marinated sufficiently, rinse it well. If you wish, you may slice it in portions at this point and freeze some of them. Slicing the final product is difficult but worthwhile. Garnish with lemon juice, dill, and pepper–and capers if desired. Makes 2 pounds.

Jane's Tex-Mex Turnovers

This recipe, which was requested by several enthusiastic diners at a recent Playhouse Party, comes from Jane Montgomery, a funny, frank woman whose family has rented at Singing Brook Farm for 40 years. It makes a LOT of turnovers; feel free to halve it for a smaller group.

for the dough:
12 ounces cream cheese
1-1/2 cups (3 sticks!) butter
3 cups flour
1-1/2 teaspoons salt

for the filling:
12 ounces cream cheese
1 whole chicken breast, poached, with skin and bones removed, diced
1 small can (4 ounces) chopped green chiles
1/2 red bell pepper, seeded and diced
5 chopped scallions (white part only)
4 ounces Monterey Jack or Cheddar cheese, shredded
1 tablespoon ground cumin
salt and pepper to taste

Mix the dough ingredients into a smooth ball, and chill for at least 1 hour.

Place all of the filling ingredients in a large mixing bowl and beat well. Do not use a food processor. Heat the oven to 350 degrees, and line a baking sheet with parchment paper. Divide the dough in half, and roll each half out until it is 1/8 inch thick. Cut each half into 5- or 6-inch squares for meal-size turnovers or smaller for snack size. Put as much filling as possible on each piece, fold into a triangle, crimp the edges, and bake until golden brown, about 25 minutes for small turnovers or 40 for large ones. Serve hot or at room temperature.

Makes 72 small, 2-bite turnovers (2-1/2 inches square) or 16 large ones.

Sate (Also Called Satay) from Indonesia

Mary Parker visited her son Harrison in Indonesia and returned to introduce Singing Brook Farm to this tasty (and fairly simple) dish. It quickly became a Farm favorite.

1-1/2 pounds flank steak (boned, skinless chicken breast may also be used)
4 tablespoons oil
2 tablespoons soy sauce
1 teaspoon salt
1 clove garlic, finely cut
1 small onion, finely cut
2 tablespoons red wine
1 teaspoon sugar

If you are using wooden skewers, soak them for at least a couple of hours in cold water before cooking so they won't burn when exposed to the heat.

Cut the beef into bite-size pieces. Marinate it in the rest of the ingredients for several hours. Load about 5 pieces onto each small stick or skewer for cooking.

Broil over charcoal or in the oven broiler for three to four minutes. Do not overcook! Serve with peanut sauce (see below) and rice. Serves 6.

Peanut Sauce

This succulent sauce is an excellent accompaniment to rice and roasted vegetables, as well as to the sate above.

1 onion, coarsely cut
2 tablespoons oil
1 cup peanut butter
1 cup water
1 tablespoon soy sauce
1 teaspoon sugar
1 tablespoon lemon juice
1 small wedge fresh ginger, finely chopped (optional)
1 to 4 teaspoons crushed red pepper

Sauté the onion in the oil until lightly brown. Add the other ingredients. Experiment with the pepper. This sauce should be HOT to the taste.

Cook for 1/2 hour over low heat to blend the flavors, stirring frequently. If the sauce becomes too thick, add more water. It should be the consistency of thick cream sauce.

Any leftovers should be stored in the refrigerator.

Aunt Fox's Carrot Soufflé

Carolyn Fox, whose family summered at the Farm for many years, now works as a tour guide in Historic Deerfield. Aunt Fox insists she can't take credit for this soufflé, which was passed on to her by someone who got it from someone else. Nevertheless, it was, as she puts it, "a frequent entrant in the Singing Brook Farm traditional pot-lucks." The recipe takes a healthy food (the carrot) and makes it as fattening (and flavorful) as possible.

2 cups cooked carrots
3 tablespoons cornstarch
1-1/4 cups light cream
1 teaspoon salt
1/4 cup honey
3 eggs, well beaten
4 tablespoons melted sweet butter

Preheat the oven to 350 degrees. Put the cooked carrots through a sieve–or puree them in a blender or food processor. Stir the cornstarch into the cream. Then add the salt, honey, and cream to the carrots. Stir in the eggs and melted butter.

Bake in a buttered casserole dish for 45 minutes. Serves 4 to 6.

Jan Weisblat's Indian Chicken Curry

My family spent many years in India and came back with dishes that have found their way to the Playhouse. This recipe was transcribed from my mother's instructions by singer Jody Kerssenbrock. Feel free to play around with spices.

4 to 6 tablespoons peanut or canola oil
1 onion, sliced and chopped
1 piece (about 1 inch long) fresh ginger, chopped
2 cloves garlic, mashed
1 chicken, cut up
1 tomato, cored and chopped
2 tablespoons curry powder
1 tablespoon chili powder
salt to taste
1 cup chicken stock, plus more as needed
2 tablespoons coconut
1 tablespoon peanut butter
the juice of 1 lemon or 1 lime

Heat the oil in a frying pan. Sauté the onion, ginger, and garlic. Brown the chicken pieces lightly; then remove them. Lower the heat, and add the tomato, curry powder, chili powder, and salt. Add enough stock to keep the mixture from burning. Cook, stirring, for 4 minutes.

Add about 1/4 cup more stock and add the chicken again. Add the coconut and peanut butter. Then stir in 1/4 cup more stock, or enough to achieve the consistency of a light gravy. Simmer the chicken, covered, until done (40 minutes to 1 hour), adding stock as necessary. Before serving, add the lemon or lime juice.

Serve with rice. Chutney, chopped peanuts, and shredded coconut make tasty condiments. Serves 4 to 6.

Bobbie's Chicken and Lemon

Bobbie Carlin is a New Yorker born and bred who spends her summers in a cottage at Singing Brook farm called–what else?–Pudding Hollow. She brought this sweet-and-sour recipe back from a visit to Captain Jack's Wharf in Provincetown, Massachusetts, in 1972. It has become a Farm favorite.

6 to 8 pieces of chicken (a fryer, cut up)
1/2 cup lemon juice
1/2 cup sifted flour
1 teaspoon salt
1 teaspoon paprika
1/4 cup vegetable oil
4 tablespoons brown sugar, firmly packed
2 lemons, thinly sliced
2 cups chicken broth

Preheat the oven to 375 degrees. Wash and drain the chicken. Rub the lemon juice on it, and shake each piece in a paper bag containing the flour, salt, and paprika.

Brown the chicken slowly in the oil. Then arrange the browned chicken pieces in a 2-quart casserole dish. Sprinkle the sugar over them and cover with the sliced lemons. Pour the chicken broth on top.

Cover and bake for 1 hour or until the chicken is tender. Serves 4 to 6.

Fresh Tomato Salad

No dish shouts "Summer!" like a plate of fresh tomatoes. Of course, you don't have to do more than throw tomatoes and some basil onto a platter, but this Playhouse version dresses up the dish a little. If you can find heirloom tomatoes, which tend to be smaller than the standard farm-stand and garden varieties, cut them into small wedges instead of slices. Feel free to vary the flavorings: go Indian with a bit of cumin, or use goat cheese instead of the Romano.

2 tablespoons pine nuts
2 large ripe, fresh tomatoes, cored and sliced
2 tablespoons coarsely chopped flat-leaf parsley
2 leaves fresh basil, chopped coarsely
sea salt and freshly ground pepper to taste
4 teaspoons extra-virgin olive oil
1 teaspoon balsamic vinegar
a sprinkle of freshly grated Romano cheese

Toast the pine nuts briefly in a small frying pan, stirring constantly and being careful not to burn them. Set them aside. Arrange the tomato slices on a platter, and cover them with the parsley and basil. Top with salt and pepper. Drizzle the oil on top, followed by the vinegar. Toss on the pine nuts and the cheese. Serve immediately.

Serves 4.

Viennese Chocolate Cherry Cake

This cake comes from Ena Haines, who along with her sister Betsy and mother Toni stayed for many years in the Singing Brook Farm cottage known as the Bungalow. Toni, now an octogenarian stock broker, trained as a chef in prewar Vienna, where she learned to make this elegant creation.

6 ounces (1 cup) semi-sweet chocolate chips
3/4 cup (1-1/2 sticks) sweet butter, at room temperature
3/4 cup sugar
5 eggs, separated
1 cup crushed Italian egg biscuits (or vanilla-wafer or graham-cracker crumbs)
1/2 of a 16-ounce can dark, sweet, pitted cherries, drained
powdered sugar as needed

Preheat the oven to 350 degrees. Melt the chocolate chips over hot water. While they are cooling, cream together the butter and sugar. Add the egg yolks, and continue beating. Add the melted, cooled chocolate.

In a separate bowl, beat the egg whites until they are stiff but not dry. Fold them into the batter alternately with the crumbs. Pour the mixture into a greased, 8-inch springform pan. Arrange the cherries on the top, and push them down into the batter just a little.

Bake for about 40 minutes. The cake is done when it springs back to the touch, but it should still be quite moist. Cool the cake and remove it from the pan. Sprinkle the top with powdered sugar. Serves 8 to 10.

Hawley Torte

The dazzling Florette came up with this fool-proof crowd pleaser. She actually makes it with a base of lady fingers rather than vanilla wafers and covers it with whipped cream, but finding myself without the fingers or cream one day I used the vanilla wafers, and I liked the results. The ingredients may seem pedestrian, but the torte is really something special.

1 box (11 ounces) vanilla wafers
6 to 8 Heath bars (1.4 ounces each)
1/2 gallon vanilla ice cream, softened
several dollops of Kahlua

Line the bottom and sides of a large casserole dish with vanilla wafers. Use parts of more wafers and wafer crumbs to fill in the holes between wafers to establish a crust.

Crush the Heath bars inside their wrappers and a plastic bag, using a rolling pin or (if you are desperate) a heavy shoe. A few large chunks are acceptable, but try to make a great many small ones. Remove the candy from the wrappers.

In a large bowl, combine the Heath-bar crumbs and the ice cream. Place this mixture inside the wafer crust. Then gently add the kahlua, but don't blend it into the ice cream too thoroughly; it should form swirls in the mixture.

Sprinkle additional vanilla wafer crumbs on top of the torte, cover it, and place it in the freezer, where it should remain for at least 6 hours. Serves 10.

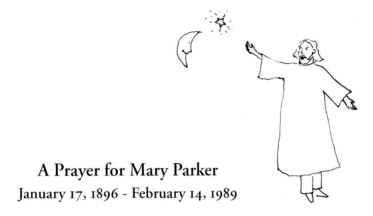

A Prayer for Mary Parker
January 17, 1896 - February 14, 1989

Mick Comstock, the pastor of the Federated Church in Charlemont, wrote this prayer/poem for Gam's memorial service. It may give you some idea of her strength and vitality—and of her effect upon those around her.

O God, when a hurricane sweeps across our shores, we do not give thanks but batten down and board up and hunker down for the duration, and then creep out to gaze with devastated awe at the great unmaking and remaking of our lives, the reshaping of our shores, the redefinition of the boundaries that join our selves to the fathomless sea.

But why do we speak of a hurricane when Mary's was an ordering wind, a creating wind, a wind of powerful loving that blew through our lives since before they began, or blew into our lives when our backs were turned, our attention elsewhere.

Some of us simply set sail and ran always before the wind and blew to wonderful places and saw marvelous things. Some of us sought safe harbor. Some of us tacked, determined to go another way, but able, still, to make use of the wind. Some of us stood on the shore, wistful, admiring. Some of us stood defiantly, facing into the teeth of it, rooted in an ordering of our own and yet our postures shaped by the wind and the defiance. Some of us found locomotion of our own and went where we would, despite the wind.

But all of us, dear God, all of us are here in this quiet place and time, gathered to give thanks and praise for the wind, glad for the blowing and the ordering and the shaping of our lives; able, at least in this moment, to say, "That's who she was. Thanks be to God! This is who we are. Thanks be to God!"

But knowing also that this quiet is the eye of the storm, and wondering what wind will blow next and how will we fare, and maybe puffing ourselves up to do a little blowing of our own.

So be with us today and in the days following, dear God, and with your healing spirit heal the wounds of the wind's passing, and with your Holy Spirit fill our sails. Amen.

The Bridge of Flowers

A Culinary Tour of Shelburne Falls

The weekly *Shelburne Falls and West County News* has published numerous editorials complaining about tourists' (and journalists') characterization of Shelburne Falls as quaint. This village is a growing, breathing community, the paper's editorial-page writers argue, not a picture-postcard scene. The writers have a point. But they're still wasting their breath and their column inches. The place is too darn charming to avoid the "quaint" epithet.

My mother, who for many years ran an antique shop near the center of the village, likes to describe Shelburne Falls as a 19th-century town in 21st-century America. Certainly, looking out of the windows of the cozy Country Dog Antique Shop (formerly my mother's shop, the Merry Lion), one sees remnants of an earlier era.

Across the way stand the volunteer fire department and an array of Victorian-built homes and shops. Down the street one can spot a 100-year-old iron bridge across the river; an old granary (now the Salmon Falls Marketplace, a craft shop and architect's office); and the picturesque Bridge of Flowers, a former trolley bridge festooned with seasonal blossoms by the local garden club.

Shelburne Falls is not a civic entity. Nestled around the Deerfield River just off Route 2, this attractive village consists of the most populous portions of two towns, Shelburne and Buckland. Despite its lack of municipal wholeness, the village enjoys a strong sense of identity.

To many, this colorful cluster of buildings and people presents an ideal situation in which to live and do business. As a residential area, Shelburne Falls avoids both the scramble of big-city life and the inaccessibility of country life. As a place of commerce, it offers more opportunities for innovation and community feeling than do malls and shopping centers.

As a result, the village has attracted a wide variety of dwellers and workers. Its simple, semi-rural setting brought a number of counter-cultural adherents to Shelburne Falls in the 1960s and 1970s. Many of them stayed on to bring up their children in the area, plying traditional trades like glass blowing, basket weaving, pottery throwing, candle making, and wood carving. By and large, they live comfortably beside financial

and political conservatives, together nurturing the public space that is one of the village's attractions.

The food in Shelburne Falls is as eclectic as its population. The village can boast of an excellent traditional grocery store on the Shelburne side of the river as well as a bustling health-food emporium in Buckland, known to many residents as the "tofu" side of the village. Restaurant fare ranges from vegetarian to frankly carnivorous, from the Fox Towne Coffee Shoppe (with real animal heads on the wall) to the more trendy Shelburne Falls Coffee Roasters coffeehouse.

Tourists are drawn to the village by attractions like the glacial potholes and the Bridge of Flowers. The greatest pleasure in visiting Shelburne Falls, however, is found in simply poking around–sticking one's head into the newsroom of the *West County News*, watching artists blow vases at North River Glass, or stopping into the Bottle of Bread pub for a bite

to eat. Visitors who stumble upon the place invariably return, cherishing Shelburne Falls as a major discovery.

Judith Russell was one of them. She arrived in Shelburne Falls late in her life–about 10 years before her death–and fell in love with it at first sight. She established a semi-permanent home there, first in a cabin she and her son Wes built, and later in my mother's shop, the Merry Lion.

In the shop, she set up her magnificent painting desk. Modeled on one owned by Grandma Moses, one of her heroes, it featured colorful art on all sides. I would have been terrified to work at it for fear that I might ruin the art, but Judy was always relaxed about it. From the desk and the shop she sketched and painted the village, paying special attention to the view of the Bridge of Flowers just outside the window of the Merry Lion. The village misses her.

Sarah's Sweet Scones

Bald Mountain Pottery showcases the efforts of potter Sarah Hettlinger, who runs the business with her husband Jim Gleason, a yoga instructor and amateur thespian. Sarah's informal vases, pots, and dishes often feature brush-stroked scenes of the Bridge of Flowers, which she can view from her shop window.

2-1/2 cups flour
2 teaspoons baking powder
1/2 teaspoon baking soda
1/2 teaspoon salt
1/2 cup (1 stick) sweet butter, cut up
1/4 cup sugar
2/3 cup buttermilk

Preheat the oven to 425 degrees. Place the flour, baking powder, baking soda, and salt in a large bowl, and stir to mix. Cut in the butter with a pastry blender or knives, or roll it in with your fingers, until it makes fine granules. Add the sugar, and toss to mix. Add the buttermilk, and stir with a fork to form a soft dough. (Add just a bit more buttermilk if you have to.) Form the dough into a ball, and place it on a lightly floured board. Knead the dough 10 to 12 times, and shape or cut it into 8 to 10 scones. Place them on a greased cookie sheet, and bake them for 10 to 12 minutes, until they turn light to medium brown on top. Remove the scones from the cookie sheet immediately, place them on a rack over a dish towel, and cover them loosely to cool before serving.

Makes 8 to 10 scones.

McCusker's Harvest Moon Cookies

McCusker's Market is the village's health-food store. Its owner/manager is Michael McCusker, a literal and figurative runner who is active in the local business association. These huge honey-sweetened, fiber-filled cookies are one of Mike's baking specialties. You may safely quarter his recipe.

4 cups honey
4 cups grated carrots
1 pound (4 sticks) sweet butter at room temperature
4 eggs
8 cups regular (not quick) uncooked oatmeal
4 cups whole-wheat flour
4 teaspoons cinnamon
2 teaspoons salt
1 teaspoon ground cloves
4 large apples, cored, peeled, and chopped
1 to 2 cups cranberries

Preheat the oven to 325 degrees. Combine the first 4 ingredients. Add the remaining ingredients and stir well. Scoop out rounds of dough with an ice-cream scoop (or a smaller implement such as a melon baller if desired), and bake on greased cookie sheets for 12 to 20 minutes, depending on the size of your cookies.

Makes about 4 dozen large cookies.

Nancy Dole's Cranberry Relish

Nancy L. Dole is one of the mainstays of Shelburne Falls, both in civic circles and as the proprietor of a used book and ephemera shop. This holiday relish captures the flavor of fresh cranberries. It comes from Nancy's grandmother's cookbook; next to it in the book appear the handwritten words "delicious made in 1937." It may be doubled easily.

1 bag (12 ounces) fresh cranberries
3 to 4 apples (Nancy prefers Cortlands)
2 large oranges
2/3 cup sugar

Wash the fruit and discard any soft cranberries. Cut up the apples and remove the seeds but leave the skins on. Cut up the oranges, and remove the seeds and ends but leave most of the orange peel on.

Put the mixture through a meat grinder or food processor. Nancy notes that you should be certain to put a large bowl on the floor under the grinder if you use one as the juice collected will all be used.

Mix the juice, ground fruit, and sugar thoroughly. Allow at least a half day for the flavors to blend at room temperature; then refrigerate. Use within a week's time. This relish serves 10 to 12 as a condiment with poultry–unless you're in Nancy's family, where they eat bowlsful at a time. She usually triples the recipe at Thanksgiving!

Shelburne Falls Coffee Roasters' Iced Latte

This refreshing beverage is made by the Coffee Roasters with Torani Italian Syrups. For availability of this product near you, call Torani at 800-775-1925. The most popular flavor latte at the Coffee Roasters is vanilla, which I happen to adore myself.

ice cubes as needed
milk as needed
2 ounces espresso
2 ounces flavored syrup

Fill a 12-ounce glass with ice, and then fill it to the top with milk. Pour the espresso and the syrup into a shaker; then add the contents of the glass. Shake briskly, and serve in a 16-ounce cup. Makes 1 latte.

Marge's Tex-Mex Dip

This recipe comes from a noted local thespian. Marjorie Appleton is the founding director of the West County Players of Shelburne Falls. She served this simple dip at a cast party and gave me the recipe. If you have time, make the dip the day before you plan to serve it to allow the flavors to blend; then refrigerate it overnight and reheat it for your party.

1 pound ground beef
1 medium onion, chopped
8 ounces pepper jack cheese, grated or cut into small cubes
4 ounces Velveeta (you may substitute about 1/2 cup grated Cheddar cheese and 1/2 cup milk)
1/2 of a 16-ounce can of refried beans
1/2 cup salsa, or more to taste (I use a full cup!)
chili powder to taste
salt to taste (I use 1 teaspoon)

Cook the ground beef and onion until the meat is brown and the onion pieces are tender. Drain. Add the other ingredients, and mix well. Heat the dip in a saucepan or microwave oven; then place it in a fondue pot and keep it warm. Serve with tortilla chips. This recipe is easy to change for different tastes, explains Marge. It can be made hot or mild. Plain Cheddar cheese or Monterey Jack without the peppers will make it mild. If it's too thick, add a little more salsa or a tablespoon of water. Serves 8 to 12.

Merry Lion Hot Fudge Sauce

When my mother decided to repaint the brown exterior of her shop. Judy and I convinced her to brighten it up with hot pink trim. Shelburne Falls has never been the same color-wise since! We decided the place looked like nothing so much as a hot-fudge sundae with peppermint-stick ice cream—and served sundaes to celebrate the occasion. Here's the simple recipe we used for the sauce.

1 cup sugar
1/4 cup cocoa
1 tablespoon sweet butter
5 ounces evaporated milk (a small can)
1/2 teaspoon vanilla

Combine the sugar and cocoa in a saucepan and heat them until they are warm to the touch. (This is the only tricky part of the recipe; make sure you stir them, or they'll burn!)

When they're hot but not melting, add the butter and the evaporated milk. Bring the mixture to a boil and boil for 1 minute, stirring frequently.

Remove from heat and stir in the vanilla. You're ready to have a sundae party! Serves 8.

At the Sign of the Merry Lion

Alan's Cider Syrup Roasted Root Vegetables with Orange Cardamom Dressing

Alan Harris is the chef and chief administrator of Noble Feast Catering. This dish is typical of Alan's menu selection; he likes to give local foods a twist. Served either hot or cold at a family or holiday gathering, the vegetables are beautiful and tasty. If you want to serve the dish warm, you may cut the quantity of dressing you make in half.

for the apple cider syrup:
1/2 gallon cider
2 cups sugar
1/2 to 1 cup (1 to 2 sticks) sweet butter (I used 1 stick, which was sufficiently rich)

for the vegetables:
2 parsnips, peeled and sliced in 1/2-inch pieces
2 carrots, peeled and sliced in 1/2-inch pieces
1 small to medium butternut squash, peeled and cut into julienne strips that measure 1/4 inch thick, 1/2 inch wide, and 2 to 3 inches long
2 sweet potatoes, peeled and cut like the squash
2 medium beets, boiled whole till tender and peeled, then sliced
salt and pepper to taste

for the dressing:
the juice of 4 oranges
the juice of 2 lemons
2 to 3 shallots, minced
1 tablespoon minced fresh thyme
1 tablespoon minced fresh flat-leaf parsley
1 teaspoon ground cardamom or cumin (not both!)
salt and pepper to taste
1 cup olive oil (or a bit more if needed)
1 tablespoon honey (optional, but good; in fact, I throw in a bit extra)

Make the syrup by boiling the cider and sugar down to 2 cups or less; reduce the mixture until bubbles thicken and it is a nice amber color and coats a spoon. (This may take as long as an hour.) Melt the butter and add it to the syrup.

Next, roast the vegetables. Coat them with the cider syrup and roast them on shallow pans in a 400-degree oven until they are tender and slightly colored. Roast the carrots and parsnips together, the squash and sweet potato together, and the beets separately. Lightly salt and pepper the vegetables.

To make the dressing, mix the juices together, then add the shallots, herbs and spice, and a light coating of salt and pepper. Whisk in the olive oil and the honey if desired.

Much of the work for this dish may be done in advance. To serve hot later, mix all of the vegetables (except the beets, which must be kept separate to keep them from bleeding onto the colors of their neighbors), reheat them in a baking pan, and serve with dressing drizzled over all. To serve cold, mix with enough dressing to coat well, and arrange on a platter. (The beets again should be mixed separately and placed in their own spot on the platter.) You may garnish the mixture with additional minced herbs if you like. Serves 8 to 10.

Mother's Black Bean Soup With (or Without) Chicken

Mother's Restaurant is a thriving concern on the Shelburne side of the village. One of Mother's specialties is soup; chef Tom DeHoyos estimates that between 150 and 200 bowls are filled daily in the small eatery. Here is one of his signature soups. Feel free to experiment. If you are serving vegetarians, omit the chicken. If you wish to enhance the spices' effect, add some of them before cooking rather than after. If you want a lighter soup, use fewer beans.

1 cup chopped onion
1 cup chopped celery
2 carrots, chopped
2 cloves garlic, chopped
oil as needed for sautéing
2-1/3 cups black beans, soaked for 24 hours (You may also use canned beans, in which case the soaking is unnecessary.)
1 quart vegetable or chicken stock
1 quart water
1 teaspoon cumin (I love cumin so I double this quantity!)
1 teaspoon oregano
1/4 teaspoon crushed coriander seed or dried coriander leaf
1 teaspoon thyme
salt and pepper to taste
1 pound cooked chicken, diced or shredded
Creole seasoning to taste
sour cream and/or shredded Cheddar cheese for garnish

In a soup pot, sauté the onion, celery, carrots, and garlic in a bit of oil for 10 to 12 minutes, or until the vegetables become limp. Add the beans and stir. Stir in the stock and water, and bring the soup to a boil; then reduce the heat and simmer partly covered, stirring occasionally, until the beans soften, about 1 to 1-1/2 hours. Stir in the cumin, oregano, coriander, thyme, salt, and pepper. Allow the mixture to cool slightly, and then puree it in a food processor. Stir in the chicken.

If you have time, let the soup sit overnight in the refrigerator (or at least for an hour or 2) to allow the flavors to blend. If you have done this, you will need to reheat the soup. Ladle it into bowls, and sprinkle on the Creole seasoning. Garnish with sour cream and/or cheese if desired. Serves 4 to 6.

The Copper Angel's Sunday Brunch Blueberry Buckwheat Pancakes

The Copper Angel Café, which closed in 2002, was run by the energetic Gail Beauregard and Nicol Wander. Nicol's angel-inspired decor complemented Gail's imaginative meals. These pancakes always brightened brunch at the Copper Angel, which was located right next to my mother's antique shop.

2 eggs
1/4 cup canola oil
4 cups buttermilk (plus a bit more if needed)
1-1/2 cups buckwheat flour
1-1/2 cups white flour
1 teaspoon baking powder
1 teaspoon baking soda
1/4 teaspoon salt
fresh blueberries as needed

Mix the eggs with the oil and then add the buttermilk. Mix together the dry ingredients, and add the wet ingredients to them; if the mixture seems a bit thick, add additional buttermilk.

Sprinkle blueberries onto your pancakes while cooking on a griddle. (If you don't happen to have any blueberries, you may serve the buckwheat cakes plain.) Top with warm maple syrup, preferably local.

Serves 8.

Guinness Pot Roast

This hearty dish was inspired by a beef stew served at A Bottle of Bread, a Shelburne Falls café and pub that gets its name from the nourishing properties of beer. Feel free to substitute and/or add other vegetables if you like—onions, parsnips, turnips, etc.

12 ounces Guinness stout
1 cup sweet cider
2 tablespoons brown sugar, firmly packed
2 teaspoons salt
lots of freshly ground pepper
1 teaspoon fresh thyme
1 tablespoon fresh, chopped parsley (plus more for garnish)
2 cloves garlic, minced
1 pot roast (about 2 pounds)
flour as needed for dredging
3 tablespoons oil or bacon fat
6 potatoes, skinned and halved
1 pound carrots, cleaned, trimmed, and sliced
4 leeks, cleaned, trimmed, and sliced (use mostly the white part)

Combine the stout, cider, sugar, salt, pepper, thyme, parsley, and garlic. Pour this marinade over the beef, and let it stand, covered, in the refrigerator for 24 hours. Turn and baste from time to time if the roast is not submerged in the liquid. Remove the roast from the marinade, reserving the juice, and sprinkle it with flour.

Heat the oil or bacon fat, and brown the meat lightly on all sides in a pot or Dutch oven. Add the marinade, bring the liquid to a boil, lower the heat, and cover tightly. Simmer for 3 hours. Add the vegetables, and simmer for another 2 hours. Sprinkle on additional parsley, and serve.

Serves 6.

Peaceable Kingdom
in My Kitchen

Listening & Eating with Mohawk Trail Concerts

Intellectuals often stress the link between mathematics and music. They argue that the mind that takes pleasure in the theorems of the one can trip easily through the glissandos of the other. To me, music's most prominent parallel field is cooking. Both food and music strike me as sensual, not intellectual, experiences. And the music makers and music lovers I know are all fans (and creators) of culinary concoctions.

A case in point is provided by the delightful summer chamber-music series based in Charlemont, Mohawk Trail Concerts. MTC began over three decades ago. One summer Sunday morning, composer/conductor Alice Parker (who bakes a mean loaf of bread) invited her friend, violinist Arnold Black (who specialized in squash pancakes), to play for a service in Charlemont's Federated Church.

Arnie Black lifted his bow to begin a Haydn concerto and quickly discovered what members of the Federated Church had known for 125 years–that the sanctuary had magnificent acoustics. The first time I sang a solo there, I was so impressed with my suddenly fabulous voice that I vowed never to sing in another auditorium. I've broken that vow since, but I never sound as good elsewhere as I do in the Federated Church!

Arnie talked to the minister, a beloved senior citizen named Hank Bartlett, and the following summer the Mohawk Trail Concert series was born. From its first concert, MTC threw musicians and community members together. Folks from the church and from the surrounding hills raised money, built stage platforms, and occasionally even performed themselves–showing that, for them as well as for the professionals, music was something you made and not just something you listened to.

Food has always been central to the Mohawk Trail Concerts experience. For many years cookies and punch after the concerts on Saturdays provided an excuse for interaction between musicians and audience members, an interaction cherished by both.

Late-night suppers for musicians on Saturday nights have allowed locals to show off their culinary skills. MTC's annual meeting provides another food fest as board members, musicians, and neighbors gather to assess the season over a pot-luck feast. At these gatherings making food and making music–eating and listening–mingle and enhance each other.

Arnie died in 2000, but the music didn't die with him. His wife Ruth (always a driving force behind the concert series) and others have continued to bring chamber music and the food that goes with it to the hilltowns.

Below I offer a taste of MTC with recipes from some of the individuals central to the success of the concert series. Be sure to listen to appropriate music as you cook and eat.

Arnie's Squash Latkes by Way of "The Steppes of Central Asia" (to be eaten to Alexander Borodin's Music of the Same Name)

Arnie attributed these vegetable pancakes to his mother, who came from Russia.

2 good-sized summer squash, grated
1 egg
2 tablespoons canola oil
1 cup milk
2 cups pancake or biscuit mix, plus a bit more if needed
sour cream as garnish

Place the grated squash in a mixing bowl and add the egg. Add the oil, the milk, and then the pancake or biscuit mix, stirring but not beating. Add a bit more mix if the batter seems runny.

Spoon the batter into pancakes on a very hot, buttered griddle. Turn when bubbles start to appear. Serve with sour cream or maple syrup or both. This recipe serves 4 but can be doubled easily.

Ruth's Rhubarb Fool

Arnie's widow Ruth combines competence, humor, and musicianship. She serves as the concerts' co-artistic director. An Englishwoman by birth, Ruth has long been a fan of edible fools. She prefers to make them with gooseberries, but in the absence of these fruits in Massachusetts she makes do with rhubarb.

1 pound young, tender rhubarb (stalks only), cleaned and cut into 1/2-inch lengths
the rind of 1 lemon, grated
1/2 cup sugar (or more to taste)
1 tablespoon water
1 cup whipping cream
more sugar to taste
mint leaves

Combine the first 4 ingredients, and cook them in the top of a double boiler, covered. Bring to a boil and simmer until thoroughly soft. Crush or mash the mixture (this may be done in a blender) until pureed but not watery. (If it is runny, pour off the watery liquid and feel free to enjoy a refreshing drink, advises Ruth.) Let the fruit cool but not become ice cold.

In a separate bowl whip the cream with a little sugar to sweeten it. Fold the cream into the fruit until prettily streaked and serve in individual glass dishes. Garnish with a mint leaf. (In the absence of gooseberry leaves, explains Ruth, mint does nicely.) Serves 6.

Alice's Bread

This basic, tasty bread stood Alice Parker Pyle in good stead years ago, when MTC was being founded, and she was trying to juggle her career and five young children. The odor of the baking bread is a happy memory of my youth. The recipe may be cut in half if you don't need four loaves; in that case, you will still want to use the whole packet of yeast.

1 quart warm water
1 package yeast (plain, dried variety)
1 cup powdered milk (optional)
1 teaspoon sugar (optional)
1 tablespoon salt, or salt to taste (optional)
about 12 cups flour

Directions:

Dump the water into a very large bowl, plastic bucket, or washtub. Have the water warm enough so that the yeast can proof in it–that is, bubble to show you it's working–but not too hot; aim for lukewarm. At this point, you may add the powdered milk and sugar; these help the yeast to work. (The powdered milk also encourages the loaves to brown later.) Let the mixture sit for a few minutes to allow the yeast to get going.

Add the salt and 9 to 10 cups of the flour. Stir with a wooden spoon until the dough won't stir anymore because it's so thick. Grease your hands, plunge them in, and keep mixing until you can't see any more flour; basically, you'll be kneading the bread in the bowl.

Your plunged fingers should eventually shape the dough into a ball that breaks away from the sides of the bowl. You may need to add more flour if the dough is too messy. Keep adding and kneading until the dough is smooth. Place the mixture in a greased mixing bowl, cover with a damp cloth, and let the dough rise for 2 to 3 hours, until it doubles in size. This timing is very loose, according to Alice.

When the rising is over, plunge your fingers back into the dough. Burst all the little bubbles, and knock it down. "Then I turn it over in the pot," says Alice "and then if I have time, I let it rise again (about half as long this time). If I don't have time, I turn it out onto a floured board."

Grease 4 bread pans. Divide the dough into 4 equal portions with a carving knife. Knead each one separately, dipping the cut, raw edges in a bit of flour to smooth them. Form each portion into a loaf. Put the side of each loaf that looks prettier down in a pan; then turn it over so that that side is now oiled and on top. "It's amazing how you can manhandle it at this point," Alice says of the dough. Cover the loaves with a damp cloth, and let them rise about 1 hour, until they look nice and curved on the top. Place them in a 400-degree oven, and bake for about 30 minutes.

To test a loaf to see whether it is done, knock on the top of it. According to Alice, "It should sound like you're knocking on wood." Remove the loaves from the oven, and turn them out onto a cooling rack. "There is no preservative in them. There is no sweetening in them. There is no shortening in them. So they taste absolutely marvelous hot," she reports. Makes 4 loaves.

Mohawk Trail Concerts Punch

This punch recipe is served at each Saturday concert—except when my mother is the punch lady; she can never resist throwing any extra beverages and fruits she has into the punch! Even without my mother's additions, this punch goes fast. It was created by Mary Parker, Alice's mother, who helped the Blacks work through many details of the concert organization in MTC's early years.

4 cans (46 ounces each) Fruit Juicy Red Hawaiian Punch
2 cans (46 ounces each) pineapple juice
9 quarts ginger ale, chilled

Put the Hawaiian Punch and juice into a large container and mix thoroughly. Divide the mixed juice into 3 containers, and chill them for at least 24 hours. When ready to serve, pour 1 container of the juice mixture into a punch bowl and add 3 quarts ginger ale to it. A block of ice may be added to the punch bowl to keep it cold. Refill as needed. Serves 100 to 120 people using 5-ounce cups.

Merry Lion MTC Punch

Here's one of the post-concert punches made by my mother, whose antique shop was called the Merry Lion. The secret is the mint syrup.

2 cups mint syrup (See page 126.)
4 cups iced tea
2 cans (46 ounces each) pineapple juice, some frozen as ice
6 quarts ginger ale
mint leaves as desired

Combine the first 3 ingredients; then pour them over ice in punch bowls until half full. Pour the ginger ale on the top at the last minute. Mint leaves floating on top make a nice garnish. Serves 50 to 75 with 5-ounce cups.

The Best Cookies

My mother and I have served these shortbread-esque cookies happily at many after-concert receptions. Originally known as "Toffee Squares," they were rechristened by my nephew Michael for obvious reasons.

1 cup (2 sticks) sweet butter, at room temperature
1 cup brown sugar, firmly packed
1 egg yolk, beaten
1 teaspoon vanilla
2 cups sifted flour
8 ounces milk chocolate, melted
blanched almonds to taste

Preheat the oven to 350 degrees. Cream the butter and sugar together until light and fluffy. Add the beaten egg yolk, vanilla, and flour. Spread this mixture onto an ungreased medium (around 10-by-14-inch) jelly-roll pan, patting it out to the edges with your fingers and palms. (They work better than a knife or spatula.) If you use a cookie sheet without sides, the dough will spill over in the oven. If you have only a large pan, don't stretch the dough to the edges; it should not be overly thin. Bake the cookies for 15 to 20 minutes, and remove them from the oven.

Quickly spread the melted chocolate over the top of the baked cookie dough. Grate almonds over all. (They will look like little snowflakes on top of the chocolate.) Cool and cut into pieces.

Makes about 36 cookies.

Bill Shea's Omelettes

Bill Shea, a former president of MTC , and his wife Janice are perennial party givers after MTC concerts–and Bill always makes individual omelettes for his guests. Bill prefers to use a pan consecrated to omelettes for his creations, but any small round or oval pan or skillet will do. If you are not using a pre-seasoned pan, he suggests spraying the pan with nonstick spray before cooking. Below is the formula for an individual omelette.

2 eggs
1 tablespoon sweet butter
thinly sliced cheese as needed
(optional–Cheddar, Swiss, Gruyere, Provolone, or
even American)
herbs to taste
salt and pepper to taste

Bring the eggs to room temperature by placing them briefly in warm water. Break the eggs into a small bowl, and beat lightly with a fork or wire whisk. Place the butter in the pan over high heat. When the butter melts and begins to turn slightly brown, pour in the eggs. Let the egg mixture sit until you count to 7, add herbs and salt and pepper, and swirl the egg mixture around the pan until the mixture builds up and sets. (I use a fork judiciously to pull in the sides of the eggs just a little and let the wet part cook at the edges.) Roll the omelette by tipping the pan and folding or rolling the side opposite the handle. Turn it onto a warm plate. Serves 1.

Bill suggests adding thinly sliced cheese just before you roll the eggs. He also likes to use a bit of whatever sauce he has in the house as a garnish at the end. When he makes omelettes for a crowd, he mixes 2 eggs per person in a large bowl with an electric beater and cooks approximately two eggs at a time. When he really gets going, the omelettes take only about a minute apiece, and he has to turn down the heat from time to time.

Helen's Roast-Beef Salad

Helen Spencer was the president of MTC for a number of years. Along with her superb organizational skills, she brought to the concerts her experience as a caterer, so her parties were always special favorites of the after-concert crowd. This elegant roast-beef salad she created with her husband Chaloner (known as Spence) is a real treat. Helen designed it to serve 40 to 50 people, but I have scaled down the recipe.

3 pounds roast beef (eye of round, cooked RARE and trimmed of all fat), cut into thick (3/8-inch) slices and julienned into thin, even strips
1/3 pound white firm mushrooms, sliced thin
1/3 red onion, sliced thin
1 large green or red bell pepper (or a mixture), cut in small chunks
3/4 to 1 cup balsamic vinegar dressing (see recipe below)
fresh spinach for underlay
1/2 pound cherry tomatoes or tomato wedges
1/2 small bunch watercress for garnish
1/2 pound feta cheese, crumbled

Marinate the beef, mushrooms, red onions, and peppers separately in the vinaigrette for several hours. Be sparing with the dressing. Prepare a platter with the spinach underlay. Arrange all the ingredients except the feta on top of the spinach, using the tomatoes and peppers for splashes of color. Garnish with watercress arranged randomly across the top. Helen suggests putting the feta in a side dish so people can help themselves; I couldn't help sprinkling it across the top before the watercress.

Serves 8 to 10.

Helen's Balsamic Vinegar Dressing

I add salt and pepper to this, particularly when using it on a green salad.

3 tablespoons good balsamic vinegar
(If you're making the dressing for a plain green salad, you may want to use just a bit more vinegar–say, 1/4 cup in all.)
1 tablespoon Dijon mustard
1 clove garlic, run through a garlic press
1 cup extra-virgin olive oil

Combine the vinegar, mustard, and garlic. Add the oil. Shake gently in a large jar to combine, but do not blend.

Makes about 1-1/2 cups.

Norton Juster's Oatmeal Pie

Norton Juster is a man of many talents. An architect, he also writes both fiction and nonfiction, and he is a long-time supporter of the concert series. His most famous children's book, The Phantom Tollbooth, *was converted into an opera by Arnie Black and Broadway lyricist Sheldon Harnick. Norton is also an expert on the history of rural women's work and as such has combed through many old periodicals and cookbooks. He adapted this recipe from one of them. The optional ingredients add to the delight; I like raisins and apples.*

1/4 cup (1/2 stick) sweet butter, at room temperature
1/2 cup sugar
1/4 teaspoon salt
1/2 teaspoon cinnamon
1/2 teaspoon cloves
1 cup maple syrup
3 eggs
1 cup regular (not quick) uncooked oatmeal
optional yet fun: raisins, chopped dates, chopped nuts, thinly sliced apples and/or pears
1 9-inch pie shell, unbaked

Preheat the oven to 350 degrees. Cream together the butter and sugar. Add the salt and spices. Stir in the syrup; then beat in the eggs, 1 at a time, beating well after each addition. Add the oatmeal and optional ingredients as desired. Pour the mixture into the pie shell, and bake for 1 hour.

Serves 6 to 8.

The Dreaded "Lime Jell-O Marshmallow Cottage Cheese SURPRISE!"

Joan Morris and her husband, William Bolcom, have been regular performers at MTC for more than 30 years. They are the audience's pet musicians. Joan says of the Federated Church, "I think it's my favorite place to perform because it's small enough that you can know so many of the audience, and they come back after the concert to say hello." She is an actress as well as a singer, charming audiences with her renditions of old and new, classical and popular, favorites. Bill is a Pulitzer Prize-winning composer who happens to be one of the world's most delightful pianists. In one of Joan's standard encore pieces, which never fails to bring down the house, she portrays the head of an illustrious ladies club who is bursting with pride about a molded concoction that no one else will touch with a ten-foot pole. Here is Joan's recipe, inspired by the song of the same name. She doesn't actually expect anyone to make it, but it's a lot of fun.

1 package lime gelatin
some cottage cheese
(1/2 cup or so, depending on just how healthy you want this to be)
baby marshmallows to taste
pimento slices to taste
pineapple rings to taste
vanilla wafers
(a few or lots, depending on whether or not there are children in the house)

Directions:

Mix the gelatin according to package directions. A large (1-quart) measuring cup is good, because you can toss in the next 2 ingredients, stir them up, and pour the result right into a festive mold. Set the mold in the refrigerator, "possibly covered if there are food aesthetes in the house whose dietary equilibrium will be upset by a color not normally in the edible spectrum."

Once the gelatin has gelled, unmold onto a plate. Get out your pimentos, pineapple rings, and so forth. "Now's your chance to show your stuff," says Joan. "Use the pimentos to artistically set off the design of the mold. The pineapple rings can be arranged in the center, and the vanilla wafers placed around the edge in a sort of shoring-up effect. Or just eaten while you contemplate what you hath wrought.

"Now as to the SURPRISE! part of this so-far textbook realization of a classic dish. We-e-ll … Bill and I were once served it with a soupçon of Creme de Menthe (didn't help).

"If I were making this for my Mom, say, I'd probably get a 1/2 pint of whipping cream, whip it up with some sugar, orange flavoring and a drop each of red and yellow food coloring and voila! Mommy heaven!

"Now to the most important part of this process, which we discovered thanks to the ingenuity of some friends in Rochester, N.Y. (a bastion of lime Jell-o-ness, as it turns out). Simply carry the plate over to the kitchen sink and scrape the contents into the garbage disposal. When you turn the disposal on you will hear the most satisfying schlllluuuurrrrp coming up from the depths. It resonates yet in my inner ear, a consummation devoutly to be wished! Bon appetit!"

The Heath Fair

Fair Weather Foods

The season that spans the months of August through October may well be my favorite in the hills near Pudding Hollow. It brings our most spectacular weather and plant colors. It is also synonymous with traditional New England fairs and fall festivals.

The first agricultural fair in the United States was organized in western Massachusetts in 1811 by Elkanah Watson of Pittsfield, through his Berkshire Agricultural Society. Mr. Watson, famous for importing merino sheep to this country, knew the value of networking. In their heyday in the late 19th and early 20th centuries, local agricultural fairs brought together farm families who had toiled in isolation for the preceding months. As they gathered to exhibit and admire livestock, produce, and handiwork, these Yankees cemented community ties, celebrated their products, and took a breather from the pace of their ordinary lives.

In many ways, their harvest celebrations looked back to the Thanksgiving days proclaimed by the Puritans of early New England, in which community members put productive activity on hold in order to congregate and express gratitude to their creator. The agricultural fairs also served as a vivid reminder of our Native American forebears' ties to the land.

Today, New Englanders live less isolated lives than our farmer foreparents; we routinely see more people and take more breaks from work than they did. Fairs and fall festivals have not lost their appeal, however.

They draw us together as communities in a way no civic activity can. They help us to remember our rural past, to celebrate those among us who still make a living on farms or through craft work. Pie sales and parades, ox draws and tag sales, 4-H Club exhibits and quilt displays encourage us to laugh, eat, and dance together.

Here I share recipes from fairs and festivals in the Pudding Hollow region. None of the fairs is unique. Nevertheless, each is eagerly anticipated by the community. Such fairs as these, and the foods served at them, draw us back from our computers and SUVs and telephones to celebrate the cycles of the earth and enjoy a season of magic, in which color and ripeness abound.

Dot Clark's Doughnuts from Hawley Day

The first festival of the summer, Hawley Day, marks the annual gathering of residents, former residents, and friends of the hamlet in which I live. About 100 people (roughly a third of the town's population) meet once a year on the grounds of the old East Hawley Church to catch up on news of the town's historical society, the Sons and Daughters of Hawley, and to pay tribute to Hawleyites who have died since the preceding summer. Every Hawley Day begins with a morning coffee klatch in which Hawleyites and friends share news and munchies. Dorothy Clark is the matriarch of a large family scattered throughout West County but particularly prevalent in Hawley. Her doughnuts, made fresh for the occasion, always grace the coffee klatch at Hawley Day. She notes that refrigerating the dough is essential.

4 cups flour
4 teaspoons baking powder
1 teaspoon baking soda
1 teaspoon salt
1 teaspoon nutmeg
1/3 cup (2/3 stick) sweet butter, at room temperature
1 cup sugar
3 large eggs
3/4 to 1 cup buttermilk
vegetable oil (I use canola) as needed for deep-fat frying

Sift together the first 5 ingredients. Cream the butter and sugar, and add the eggs, 1 at a time, beating well. Add the buttermilk. Gradually stir in the dry ingredients. Chill the dough overnight in a covered bowl in the refrigerator.

In the morning, knead the dough slightly, and roll it out to a thickness of 1/4 inch on a floured board. Cut it into doughnuts and deep fry them in oil at about 375 degrees. Drain the pastries on heavy brown paper while still warm. (They are delicious with a bit of spiced sugar sprinkled on top.)

Makes 24 doughnuts, more or less, depending on the size of your doughnut cutter.

Gingerbread Ring Cake from the Shelburne Grange Fair

The one-day Shelburne Grange Fair is designed to celebrate the fruits of local labors. One of the fair's joys is the competition for prizes. One year Judy won a blue ribbon for a whimsical papier-mâché pumpkin house that took days to design and construct! This basic, tasty cake won a prize for Marie Pfisterer of Shelburne.

4 cups flour
2-1/2 teaspoons ground ginger
2 teaspoons baking soda
1/2 teaspoon salt
1/2 teaspoon ground cinnamon
1 cup (2 sticks) sweet butter, at room temperature
3/4 cup dark brown sugar, firmly packed
1-1/3 cups molasses
2 eggs
1 cup hot water

Preheat the oven to 350 degrees. Grease a 10-inch bundt pan. Combine the dry ingredients. In a large bowl, beat the butter and brown sugar together. Stir in the molasses, the eggs, the dry ingredients, and then the water.

Pour the batter into the pan, and bake the cake for 45 to 50 minutes, or until a toothpick inserted into the center comes out clean. After a few minutes, loosen the cake from the pan and cool it on a wire rack.

This cake may be eaten plain, sprinkled with confectioner's sugar, or drizzled with a simple glaze and decorated. Serves 10.

Dot's Sour Cream Coffee Cake from the Federated Church Auction

The Charlemont Federated Church holds a fund-raising auction each fall. Church members always include a bake sale in the proceedings–and Dottie Purinton's sour-cream coffee cake is a perennial favorite.

1/2 cup chopped nuts (walnuts or pecans)
1 teaspoon cinnamon
1-1/2 cups sugar
2 cups flour
1 teaspoon baking powder
1 teaspoon baking soda
1/2 cup (1 stick) sweet butter, at room temperature
2 eggs, well beaten
1 cup sour cream
1 teaspoon vanilla

Preheat the oven to 350 degrees. Mix together the nuts, the cinnamon, and 1/2 cup of the sugar. Set aside. Sift together the flour, baking powder, and baking soda. Mix together the butter, remaining sugar, and eggs. Add the flour mixture, and then the sour cream and vanilla. Beat the mixture together; then pour half of it into a greased 10-inch tube pan. Spread half of the nut topping over the cake mixture, and add the remaining cake batter. Then spread on the rest of the nut topping. Bake for 45 minutes. Cool the cake in the pan before removing. Serves 10.

Donovan Baby Red Potato Salad from the Charlemont Riverfest

Riverfest is an all-day festival, highlighting the uses (and occasionally the abuses) of the Deerfield River. Situated on the banks of that river, it offers educational exhibits as well as water races and games. The Riverfest in Charlemont used to take place annually but seems to come and go a bit; luckily, Shelburne Falls also has an annual Riverfest to gladden river lovers. A few years back the Donovan Farm donated a huge pile of baby red potatoes to a Riverfest lunch. The resulting salad was very popular. I have scaled it down to feed a less than Riverfest-size crowd.

1-1/2 pounds new red potatoes
1/3 cup finely chopped red onion
2 eggs, hard boiled and chopped
2 tablespoons fresh dill (or 2 teaspoons dried dill)
25 pitted ripe olives, sliced (more if desired), plus a few olives for garnish
1 cup sour cream
1 teaspoon Dijon mustard
2 tablespoons vinegar, preferably herbal
salt and pepper to taste
3 pieces of bacon, cooked and crumbled

Wash but do not peel the potatoes. Place them in a saucepan and cover them with cold, salted water. Bring the water to a boil and cook the potatoes until they are soft enough to be pierced by a fork. Remove the potatoes from the water and cool them.

Chop the potatoes and combine them, in a medium-sized bowl, with the onion, eggs, dill, olives, sour cream, mustard, vinegar, salt, and pepper. Refrigerate for at least 6 hours. When you are ready to serve the salad, sprinkle the bacon and additional sliced (or halved) olives on top. Serves 4 to 6.

Pat's Prizewinning Oatmeal-Raisin Cookies from the Heath Fair

The Heath Fair, the biggest local festival, falls in mid-August and rivals county fairs in scope and length. Founded in 1916 "to increase community feeling and to advance community welfare," it takes up a three-day weekend and marshals the energies of almost everyone in Heath. Heathens celebrate by corralling animals of all sizes and displaying vast quantities of food and flowers. In years gone by, the Heath Fair gloried in an event called "the Speaking," in which an orator addressed and enlightened fairgoers. Well known summer Heathens like theologian Reinhold Niebuhr and Justice Felix Frankfurter participated in this rite, unfortunately no longer practiced. The versatile Pat Leuchtman won a prize at the fair several years back with these hearty cookies. At one time Pat, who has raised five children, regularly doubled or even tripled the recipe.

1-1/2 cups flour
1/2 teaspoon baking soda
1 teaspoon cinnamon
1/2 teaspoon salt
1 cup sugar
2 cups regular (not quick) uncooked oatmeal
1 cup (2 sticks) melted sweet butter, cooled a bit
2 tablespoons molasses
1 egg, beaten
1/4 cup milk
3/4 cup chopped walnuts
3/4 cup raisins

Preheat the oven to 350 degrees. Mix all the dry ingredients in a large bowl. Stir in the butter, the molasses, and the egg beaten into the milk. Mix well. Add the nuts and raisins. Drop by teaspoonful onto a greased cookie sheet. Bake the cookies until the edges are browned, about 10 to 12 minutes.

Makes about 5 dozen small cookies.

Colcannon from the Coleraine Village Fair

Every fall, the town of Colrain holds what it calls the Coleraine Village Fair, in which it celebrates the season and pays tribute to its sister town of Coleraine in Northern Ireland. Michael Collins, chef at the Green Emporium Café and Gallery, has served this tasty traditional Irish dish at the festival. He adapted it from his mother's recipe.

5 pounds potatoes (older potatoes are best because they're a bit more starchy, says Mike; do not use thin-skinned red or white)
3 to 4 quarts of water (enough to cover the spuds)
5 to 6 leeks
1 medium head cabbage
1 teaspoon salt (about)
black pepper to taste
1/8 teaspoon nutmeg
1/4 pound (1 stick) sweet butter
1/2 pint heavy cream

Skin the potatoes and cut them into quarters. Place them in the water. Slice the leeks on the bias, wash them, and discard all but the light green and white parts. Cut them into strips about 2 inches long, and add them to the potatoes. Wash, de-core, and slice the cabbage into small wedges; add these as well. Add the salt. Boil slowly for about 45 minutes, uncovered. "Everything should be kind of mushy," says Mike. After 1/2 hour, preheat the oven to 450 degrees. When the boiling is complete, drain most of the water out. Add the pepper and nutmeg, and mash with a potato masher. Do not mash until nothing is left; you'll want the dish a bit chunky. Do NOT use a food processor! Add the butter and cream. Place the mixture in a baking dish and bake for about 20 minutes, or until brown on top.

Serves 8 to 12.

Colcannon may also be served unbaked; it makes a useful side dish with just a bit of butter. Michael serves his Colcannon with ham on the side. I suggest crumbling some bacon on the top.

Apple Pound Cake from Conway's Festival of the Hills

Each fall the town of Conway hosts what it calls the Festival of the Hills. This rich cake with a caramel glaze celebrates the mature flavors of that event. It comes from Conway's Martha Harrington, who serves it to guests at her homey Nestle Inn. She recommends dishing it up with a dollop of whipped cream.

1/2 cup apple slices (peeled), plus 2 cups pared and shredded apples
3 cups flour
1 teaspoon baking soda
1 teaspoon salt
1 teaspoon cinnamon
1-1/2 cups oil (Martha uses corn oil)
2 cups white sugar
3 eggs
2 teaspoons vanilla
1 cup finely chopped pecans
1/2 cup (1 stick) sweet butter
1/2 cup brown sugar, firmly packed
2 tablespoons milk

Grease and flour a 10-inch tube pan. Preheat the oven to 325 degrees. Arrange the apple slices in a overlapping pattern on the bottom of the pan.

Combine the flour, baking soda, salt, and cinnamon. Set aside. In a large bowl, beat together the oil, white sugar, eggs, and vanilla. Gradually beat the flour mixture into the oil mixture until the combination is smooth.

Fold in the shredded apple pieces and the pecans, and turn the batter into the prepared pan. Bake for about 1 hour and 20 minutes. Cool the cake for 20 minutes, and remove it from the pan.

To prepare the topping, bring the butter, brown sugar, and milk to a boil, stirring constantly. Spoon the hot mixture over the cooled cake, allowing it to run down the sides. (It gets absorbed better if you stick holes in the cake with a fork before spooning.) This cake tastes even better the next day, says Martha.

Serves 10 to 12.

Lena LaBelle's Applesauce Cake from the Ashfield Fall Festival

The Ashfield Fall Festival, which spreads out through the sizable town of Ashfield on Columbus Day weekend, specializes in crafts. My favorite food in the festival is the ambrosial maple cotton candy. Unable to replicate that, I decided to pay tribute to the festival by featuring a fall recipe from one of Ashfield's better known families, the LaBelles. This autumnal LaBelle recipe actually hails originally from just over the Hawley-Ashfield border, where Lena LaBelle lived as a child. The old LaBelle Farm in Hawley is so close to Ashfield, and the recipe so suited to festival time (how can you have fall without apples?), that I'm tucking it in anyway. It's unlike any other applesauce cake I've ever had; the orange gives it extra zing. Lena's niece Alice Godfrey provided the recipe.

2 cups flour
1 teaspoon baking powder
1/2 teaspoon salt
1 teaspoon cinnamon
1/2 teaspoon cloves or nutmeg
1 orange
1/2 cup shortening (Alice uses Crisco; I prefer sweet butter at room temperature)
1/2 cup brown sugar, firmly packed
1/2 cup white sugar
2 eggs
1 cup applesauce
1 teaspoon baking soda
1/2 cup raisins
1/2 cup chopped nuts

Preheat the oven to 350 degrees. Combine the flour, baking powder, salt, and spices. Grind up the orange, with the rind but without the seeds, in a meat grinder or food processor. Cream the shortening and the sugars together; then beat in the eggs. Mix together the applesauce and baking soda; then stir them into the shortening mixture. Stir in the flour mixture; then fold in the orange, the raisins, and the nuts.

Bake in a greased 10-inch bundt or tube pan for about 1 hour, or until a toothpick inserted into the cake comes out clean.

This moist cake serves 10 to 12.

Ashfield Farm House

Donovan Cabbage Potato Soup from Hawley Farm & Field Day

In its bicentennial year Hawley went beyond Hawley Day's midsummer festivities and tried a foliage-oriented celebration as well, the Hawley Farm and Field Day. Potato farmer Cinni Donovan organized the event—and came up with this delicious fall soup to take advantage of her farm's produce. I make it with chicken stock as indicated; she uses an herbal broth to render the recipe vegetarian.

6 cups chicken broth
2 cups shredded green cabbage
2 cups sliced organic yellow Finn potatoes
(or other yellow potatoes)
4 tablespoons chopped fresh parsley
grated Cheddar cheese for garnish

Bring the broth to a boil. Add all the other ingredients except the cheese. Cover and boil for 1 hour, or until the potatoes are soft and the cabbage is very tender. Gently mash the soup with a hand-held potato masher to disperse the potatoes and thicken the broth. Leave some potato pieces whole if you prefer a chunkier soup.

Place in bowls and sprinkle cheese on top.

Serves 3 to 4.

Apple Cider Chicken from Cider Day

The final festival each autumn in West County is the Cider Tour, which falls on the first weekend in November. This event is the brainchild of Judith Maloney at West County Winery in Colrain, an enterprise that specializes in fruit wines and hard ciders. Judith sees hard-cider making as a natural process in the local hills and climate. "This is the time when the leaves start to fall, and New Englanders become winter hoarders," she says of the late fall. "It's a way of preparing for hibernation. I really like that sense of hoarding. Hard cider speaks to the hilltown self-sufficiency." Hard-cider making, a staple of early New England culture and cuisine, lost its prominence in this region and throughout the United States during the 19th century. As industry replaced agriculture in providing Yankees' main source of income, and as the temperance movement began to challenge the healthiness of cider, home cider making grew rarer. In recent years, however, the practice has undergone a renaissance, thanks to cider makers like Judith and her husband Terry. This elegant chicken dish was served by Chef Michael Collins at the Green Emporium during a recent Cider Tour. If you are in the area, stop in at the winery; its telephone number is 413-624-3481. If you are looking for a cider maker in your own neighborhood, try the Cider Day web site (www.ciderday.org), which lists participants in the previous year's cider events. Or call your local winery and ask for advice.

4 chicken breasts, boned, skinned, and halved (not too thick; you may use cutlets if you wish)
1 tablespoon sweet butter
1 tablespoon extra-virgin olive oil
salt and pepper to taste
1 cup hard cider
1 cup chicken stock
1 teaspoon fresh or 1/2 teaspoon dried thyme
1 cup heavy cream
1 apple, pared and sliced (a "harder" apple, like a Granny Smith or Northern Spy)
chopped parsley to taste

Slowly sauté the chicken breasts in the butter and oil until they are quite brown. While browning, sprinkle the chicken with the salt and pepper. Remove the chicken and put it aside. Deglaze the pan with the hard cider and chicken stock; then add the thyme. Simmer to reduce the liquid by half; it will become delightfully aromatic.

Add the cream and the chicken. Reduce the liquid again over low heat until it becomes slightly thick and turns a gentle brown; it should thicken slowly. If the chicken looks as though it may get too dry during this reduction, remove it briefly and slice it thinly before returning it to the liquid; it will absorb the liquid better in smaller pieces. Just before serving, add the apple pieces to the chicken; Mike explains that you want them to be a little crunchy. Turn off the heat, and let the dish sit for about 5 minutes. Garnish with a bit of parsley. Serve with rice, potatoes, couscous, or whatever strikes your fancy. Serves 4.

Golden Days in Heath

Growing Older with Gourds

Our culture tends to foster depression in those hitting middle age. The late summer and early autumn years of our lives are viewed in much of our popular culture as the gateway to decay, a time of life in which Americans (especially American women) struggle vainly to stave off the aging process.

If we take time away from the anti-middle-age themes of our television sets and fashion magazines to see and taste nature's view of this stage of life, however, we open ourselves to an entirely different message.

In nature's late summer and early autumn, our surroundings seem to glory in their transition into maturity—especially in New England, where we are blessed with seasons that stand up and shout their presence. Rich colors run riot through the landscape, and fruits and vegetables swell up with pride in their continued growth.

To me the gourd family best embodies the idea of happy middle-age. Pumpkins puff up and out, laughing as their wrinkles grow bigger and bigger, and giving extended pleasure with their deep, dark color and thick flesh. Cucumbers and squashes spread their tendrils in all directions, making the most of their final weeks by reaching out to touch every other plant they sense in the garden.

Gourds seem to delight in their bizarre shapes, doing their best to step out of the mold and amuse themselves and us with new formations. (Think of the vegetable that must have a name but which I always call "flying-saucer squash" because of its resemblance to a vehicle in a low-budget science-fiction movie.) They also play constantly with new colors and textures, creating vegetable art out of their age spots.

And they reward their cooks and eaters for their patience by providing warm, substantial dishes to stave off the chill on cooling nights.

The next time you feel like bemoaning the onset of middle age, try some gourd role-playing. Relax and enjoy the fleshy expansion that represents strength. Take credit for the wisdom that accompanies your wrinkles.

Reach into your roots and out to your friends. Savor the still warm daytime sun. Appreciate the crisp evening air that makes you glad that you—like the pumpkin—are just a little plumper, a little riper, than you were.

The following recipes are designed to evoke the joys of middle age as experienced through gourds. I don't know of any way to cook the flying-saucer squash; I tend to use it and other particularly entertaining gourds for decor. I have some delicious recipes that show off some of its relatives, however.

Maple-Baked Acorn Squash

This recipe comes from my mother (and her mother and so on), one of the best people I know for adjusting to middle age, or to any age for that matter. She is a bright, busy, matter-of-fact person who can find fun in everything. In many ways, she resembles this simple-to-prepare dish: she's warm but just a little nutty.

2 smallish acorn squash
4 pinches salt
2 to 4 tablespoons sweet butter
a few pecans, walnuts, or butternuts (optional)
a handful of raisins (optional)
maple syrup to taste
a small amount of water

Preheat the oven to 350 degrees. Cut the squash in half, lengthwise, and remove and discard the gunk and the seeds in the middle. Place the 4 halves in a baking dish, open side up. Put a pinch of salt in the well of each squash half, dab in butter, and tuck in the nuts and/or raisins if desired. Drizzle maple syrup over these ingredients. Then pour water into the pan around the squash halves to steam them; the water should come up about 1/2 inch from the bottom of the pan. Bake for 45 minutes to an hour, depending on the size of the squash. The flesh will be tender when done. Serves 4.

Cold Zucchini Soup

This delicious soup, a favorite of all mature women and men at Singing Brook Farm, brightens a warm summer or fall day. It may also be served warm if there's a chill in the air.

2 tablespoons sweet butter
1 pound zucchini, washed, stemmed, and sliced about 1/4-inch thick
1 large clove of garlic, pressed or chopped
6 small scallions, chopped
1 cup chicken broth
3/4 cup milk
salt and pepper to taste
2 teaspoons cumin
2 tablespoons fresh chopped parsley

In a largish frying pan, melt the butter, and add the zucchini, garlic, and scallions. Sauté until the zucchini is soft. Place this mixture in a blender, and add the remaining ingredients. Blend until the soup is smooth. Chill before dishing up with a dollop of sour cream or yogurt (if desired).

Serves 4.

Polly's Pumpkin Soup

This recipe comes from the repertoire of Polly Bartlett, a resident of Buckland who is always on the go. Like Polly, this pumpkin soup seems quite straightforward but is actually a subtle blend of ingredients.

for the soup:
1/2 cup diced onions
10 to 12 ounces mushrooms, washed and sliced
sweet butter for browning
3 tablespoons flour
2 teaspoons curry powder
3 cups chicken broth
1 pound cooked or canned pumpkin
1 tablespoon honey
a dash of nutmeg
salt and pepper to taste
2 cups half and half, evaporated milk, or mixed regular and powdered milk

for the green sauce:
1 cup plain yogurt
chopped chives, parsley, and green onions

for additional garnish:
oven-roasted pumpkin seeds (optional)

In the bottom of a big pot, brown the onions and mushrooms in butter. Stir in the remaining soup ingredients except the half and half (or milk), in the order indicated, and simmer for 15 minutes. Throw in the half and half (or milk) and heat just until warm. Mix the green sauce ingredients together and put a dollop of the sauce on top of the soup in each bowl.

If you have used fresh rather than canned pumpkin for your soup, you may want to rinse, drain, and then roast the seeds for an additional festive garnish; they should be placed on a thin layer of oil on a cookie sheet or iron skillet and baked for 1 hour at 250 degrees. Stir every 15 minutes, and sprinkle salt to taste over the seeds after 45 minutes.

Serves 6 to 8.

Zucchini Chocolate Cake

Frequently, the Shelburne Grange Fair sponsors a cake contest, an event that tests contestants' baking skills by asking all of them to prepare exactly the same recipe. This recipe is adapted from one used in a Grange Fair contest. The zucchini makes it a truly moist cake, tasty served plain and heavenly covered with cream-cheese frosting.

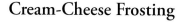

2-1/2 cups sifted flour
1/4 cup cocoa
1 teaspoon baking soda
1 teaspoon salt
1/2 cup (1 stick) sweet butter, at room temperature
1/2 cup canola oil
1-3/4 cups sugar
2 eggs
1 teaspoon vanilla
1/2 cup buttermilk
2 cups grated zucchini

Preheat the oven to 325 degrees. Sift together the flour, cocoa, baking soda, and salt, and set aside. Using an electric mixer at medium speed, cream together the butter, oil, and sugar in a mixing bowl until light and fluffy. Beat in the eggs, 1 at a time, beating well after each addition, and beat in the vanilla. Next, add the dry ingredients alternately with the buttermilk, blending well after each addition. Stir in the zucchini.

Pour the batter into a greased 13-by-9-inch baking pan. Bake for 50 minutes, or until a toothpick inserted into the cake comes out clean. Serves 16.

Cream-Cheese Frosting

My cousin Debbie Smith learned how to make this icing while working in the kitchen at her college. The butter makes it deadly—and delicious.

8 ounces cream cheese, at room temperature
1/2 cup (1 stick) sweet butter, at room temperature
2 teaspoons vanilla
1 cup confectioner's sugar (or more as needed)
milk if necessary to stir

Cream together the cream cheese and butter, and stir in the vanilla, sugar, and milk if needed. Add more confectioner's sugar to taste, but try not to overwhelm the rich cream-cheese butter combination. Frosts 1 zucchini cake.

Zucchinipalooza Zucchini Spice Brownies

In 2002 Susan and Peter Purdy of Hawley and New York City inaugurated an August event called Zucchinipalooza to celebrate the late-summer abundance of this green squash. Zucchinipalooza features a number of games (with teams called zoo, key, and knee), from squash croquet to bobbing for zucchini. Naturally, many zucchini dishes are consumed at the event. Joanne Belair of Charlemont brought these chocolatey squares the first year. A self-confessed chocoholic, Joanne likes to tweak the recipe up a bit by adding even more cocoa and chocolate chips.

1/2 cup (1 stick) sweet butter, at room temperature
1/4 cup canola oil
1-3/4 cups sugar
2 eggs
1 teaspoon vanilla
1/2 cup sour milk
(this can be created by adding a little lemon juice or vinegar to regular milk and allowing the mixture to sit for 10 minutes)
2-1/2 cups flour
1/4 cup cocoa
1/2 teaspoon cinnamon
1/2 teaspoon cloves (optional)
1/2 teaspoon baking powder
1/2 teaspoon baking soda
2 cups finely diced, ground, or grated zucchini
1-1/2 cups chocolate chips

Preheat the oven to 325 degrees. Grease and flour a 9-by-13-inch pan.

Cream together the butter, oil, and sugar. Add the eggs, vanilla, and milk, and mix well. Combine the flour, cocoa, cinnamon, cloves (if desired), baking powder, and baking soda. Gently stir them into the first mixture. Fold in the zucchini. Pour the batter into the baking pan, and sprinkle the chocolate chips on top.

Bake for 40 to 50 minutes, or until a toothpick inserted into the cake comes out clean. (Be careful not to insert the toothpick into a chocolate chip, or it will never come out clean!)

Makes 24 brownies, more or less, depending on how large you cut them.

Pudding Hollow Emilianna Relish

Here's another Zucchinipalooza entry. George McMullin, who lives smack in the heart of Pudding Hollow, presented a jar of this relish to every Zucchinipalooza guest in 2002. George says he got the recipe from Emmy Streeter of Ashfield. He makes pints and pints of this sweet-and-sour concoction every summer to take advantage of his large zucchini crop. If your garden is smaller than his, you may cut the recipe in half or even further. Just be sure to reduce the cooking time a bit; 20 minutes will do. George grinds the vegetables he puts in the relish, but I prefer to chop them into tiny pieces to give the final result a meatier consistency.

12 cups chopped zucchini
4 cups chopped onion
2 large red bell peppers, chopped
2 large green bell peppers, chopped
5 tablespoons salt
2-1/2 cups cider vinegar
1 tablespoon dry mustard
3/4 tablespoon cornstarch
1-1/2 teaspoons celery seed
4 to 5 cups sugar, depending on how sweet you like your relish
3/4 teaspoon nutmeg
1/2 teaspoon ground black pepper
3/4 teaspoon turmeric

The day before you want to make the relish, combine the vegetables and salt. Cover them with water, and let the mixture stand overnight.

The following day, rinse and drain the vegetables. Combine the remaining ingredients, and cook them until they are thick. Add the vegetables, and cook the relish for 30 minutes. Ladle it into sterilized jars. If you wish, you may process the jars for 10 minutes. (See "About Processing," page 123.)

Makes about 6 pints.

Janice Shea's Zucchini Bread

Janice Shea is a dynamic red-head who works in her husband's office, is active in her church, does volunteer work for such organizations as Mohawk Trail Concerts, and keeps tabs on her many red-headed children. She gave me this recipe years ago; I have adapted it slightly.

1 cup canola oil
1-1/2 cups brown sugar, firmly packed
3 eggs
3 cups flour
1 teaspoon baking soda
1 teaspoon salt
1 tablespoon cinnamon
1 teaspoon baking powder
2 cups grated raw zucchini
1 cup raisins
1 cup chopped nuts (optional)

Preheat the oven to 350 degrees. Combine the oil and sugar, and beat in the eggs. Combine the dry ingredients and add them to the previous mixture. Stir in the zucchini, raisins, and nuts (if desired). Bake in greased loaf pans for 45 to 60 minutes. Makes 2 loaves.

Maple-Glazed Butternut Squash

This dish is a favorite of Tom McCrumm of Ashfield, head of the Massachusetts Maple Producers Association. Tom appealingly blends sweet and savory flavors, and his final instructions reveal that he has the temperament of a tough, funny gourd. If you have a sweet tooth (as I do), you may use additional maple syrup.

1 small to medium butternut squash, peeled, seeded, quartered, and cut into 1/2-inch slices
4 tablespoons maple syrup
1/4 teaspoon ground mace
4 tablespoons dark rum
2/3 cup water

Place all of the ingredients in a large saucepan. Bring the mixture to a boil, and simmer it until the squash is tender (15 to 30 minutes). Reserve the cooking liquid. With a slotted spoon, transfer the squash to a heated serving dish. Boil the cooking liquid until it thickens, and pour it over the squash. Serves 4 to 6.

"Drink the rest of the bottle of rum, go snowmobiling over to Pudding Hollow Road, get stuck in a snowbank, walk home, sober up on the way!" says Tom.

Summer Cheddar Muffins

These cheesy, zucchini-enriched muffins come from the larder of Joanne Glier of Shelburne.

3 cups flour
4 teaspoons baking powder
1-1/2 teaspoons salt
1/2 teaspoon baking soda
1-1/4 cups grated sharp Cheddar cheese
1 cup grated zucchini
3 tablespoons chopped fresh parsley
2 to 3 tablespoons chopped scallions
2 eggs
1 cup buttermilk
1/4 cup (1/2 stick) melted sweet butter
dried (or fresh) dill to taste

Preheat the oven to 350 degrees. Sift the dry ingredients together into a large bowl. Add the cheese, zucchini, parsley, and scallions, and toss lightly to mix.

In another bowl, beat the eggs, and then whisk in the buttermilk and melted butter. Add the wet ingredients to the flour-zucchini mixture. Stir just enough to blend.

Spoon the batter into buttered muffin tins, filling them about 3/4 full. Sprinkle the muffins with dill. Bake for 30 to 35 minutes, or until golden. Cool briefly; then remove from pan. Makes about 20 muffins.

Teri's Pumpkin Cake

My graduate-school friend Teri is an extravagant, vivacious artist who dresses in bright colors and knows something about almost every subject under the sun. Like her cake, she looks a bit flaky but is in fact very substantial.

1-1/2 cups canola oil
2 cups sugar
3-1/8 cups flour
2 teaspoons cinnamon
2 teaspoons allspice
1 teaspoon salt
2 teaspoons baking powder
2 teaspoons baking soda
2 cups mashed pumpkin
4 eggs
1 teaspoon vanilla
1 cup chopped walnuts or pecans
1 cup raisins

Preheat the oven to 350 degrees. Mix the oil and sugar in a large bowl. Combine 3 cups of the flour with the other dry ingredients, and add them to the oil and sugar along with the pumpkin. (Reserve the remaining flour.) Add the eggs 1 at a time, beating well after each addition. Beat in the vanilla.

In a separate bowl, mix the remaining 1/8 cup flour with the nuts and raisins. Add them to the batter. Spoon into a greased, 10-inch bundt pan. Bake for 1 hour, or until a toothpick inserted into the cake comes out clean. Frost with raisin frosting.

Serves 10 to 12.

Teri's Secret Raisin Frosting

This icing is a bit tricky. It can almost burn if you don't stir carefully. It looks a little strange and lumpy as it goes on the cake, but the texture of the final product is one of its joys. My friend Peter says it should be called "Teri's Much Adored Raisin Frosting" because he can't eat enough of it.

1 cup evaporated milk
1 cup sugar
3 egg yolks, slightly beaten
1/2 cup (1 stick) sweet butter
1 teaspoon vanilla
1 cup raisins (plus a few more if you can't resist; I usually just throw them in impulsively)
1 generous handful coconut

Combine the first 5 ingredients in a saucepan. Cook over medium heat for 12 minutes, stirring constantly. Remove from heat. Stir in the raisins and coconut. Let the frosting stand for a minute (or maybe 2 or 3) to cool slightly.

Spoon and spread it generously over your pumpkin cake.

Why I Make Jelly

or

What's a Smart Girl Like Me Doing in a Kitchen Like This?

My graduate-school professors sometimes "tsk" on the phone and in letters when we discuss my career since my return home to the environs of Pudding Hollow. To their chagrin, my doctorate in American studies has not led to a serious teaching position.

Instead, I make my living as a freelance writer of popular (often perceived as non serious) journalism. Worse yet, during the summer for many years I prepared jellies, jams, and vinegars to sell in my mother's antique shop in Shelburne Falls.

I gravitated into my mini-career as a jelly maker when I was establishing my first contacts with newspapers and magazines. At that time, ANY spare cash proved welcome—and cash could hardly have been more spare than the income from my food business.

My writing work and income eventually enjoyed an upswing. Nevertheless, until my mother retired and sold her shop I happily welcomed the summer jelly season and maintained my kitchen sideline. As each new fruit, vegetable, and herb came into season, I would take a day or two off from writing to engage in a flurry of picking and processing.

I passed from rhubarb to strawberries, strawberries to raspberries, raspberries to blueberries, and blueberries to peaches; then I moved on to apples and quinces, with detours through herbs, tomatoes, and peppers along the way. Some of my concoctions originated in my garden. I also frequented farms that allowed me to pick my own produce.

I gained tremendous satisfaction from my kitchen work, in part because of its contrast with my writing. Jelly making is physical labor with almost immediate results; there are no rough drafts in the kitchen.

Making my products also soothed me and gave me time to reflect on my scholarship and journalism—to think through the effects of the industrial revolution on American slavery, say, or to analyze the causes of the divorce between Lucille Ball and Desi Arnaz.

In addition, my kitchen work provided me with a creative outlet. I firmly believe that everyone should engage in some artistic activity. Unfortunately, my hands are clumsy, and I can neither draw nor sculpt. Nevertheless, in conjunction with a stove and a bunch of herbs or fruits I could and can create a thing of beauty.

As I cooked, I also enhanced my awareness of the cycles of nature and my appreciation of its large and small miracles; the colors of my jellies and vinegars provided me with a constant source of wonder.

Above all, my jelly making forged and forges a link between me and other people, in the past and in the present.

As I chop, stir, boil, and process, I feel a kinship with my mother, my grandmother, and a long line of New England cooks. These homebodies spent large portions of their lives capturing the warmer seasons in jars and bottles to cheer up their families' cold-weather pantries and tables.

Through my jelly making I also cultivate closer ties to many of my rural neighbors. Few of them have been to graduate school, and few appreciate or even understand much of my critical and analytical writing. Most don't give a darn about the industrial revolution or even (heaven forbid!) Lucy and Desi's status as cultural icons.

They can relate to gardening and jelly making, however, and to the tasks those enterprises involve–from mulching beds with newspapers to stirring jelly just before putting it into jars. They have shared their cooking techniques with me and thereby shared their lives.

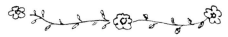

Pepper Jelly

This jelly was my strongest-selling product. Pepper jelly has only hit the northeast in the past decade or so, although it has long been a staple in southern kitchens. If you want to get the full southern effect, try it on the side of black-eyed peas; otherwise, spread cream cheese on a cracker and spoon a bit of jelly on top. You may use either red or green bell peppers for this spread; if possible, I prefer the red as they lend it a stunning color. One hint: be sure to wear rubber gloves as you seed and chop the hot peppers. I once used my bare hands and later touched my face–ouch!

3 medium bell peppers, seeded and coarsely chopped
2 2-inch jalapeño or cayenne peppers (more, if you're adventurous!), seeded and chopped
1-1/2 cups distilled white vinegar
6-1/2 cups sugar
a dab of sweet butter
2 pouches (6 ounces) liquid pectin

Chop the peppers, and blend them with 1 cup of the vinegar in a blender or food processor. Pour the blended mixture into a large non-aluminum pot and stir in all the other ingredients except the pectin. Bring the mixture to a full, rolling boil, stirring frequently; then stir in the pectin. Boil for 1 minute, stirring constantly, then remove from heat. Skim off any foam; there shouldn't be much as the butter serves to keep it down. Stir the mixture for 5 minutes to distribute the chopped peppers evenly; then ladle it into sterilized jars. Place the jars in a boiling-water bath and process for 5 minutes. (See "About Processing," page 123.) Makes 5 to 6 cups.

About Processing

Several of the recipes in this chapter, and elsewhere in *The Pudding Hollow Cookbook*, require processing of jars for such canned goods as jellies and preserves. The best way to learn about canning is to consult the excellent guides put out by the U.S. Department of Agriculture on this subject, which may be sent for in writing or found online. I urge readers to peruse these guides if they have not canned before. As a brief introduction to the topic, I am describing the process I personally follow for canning.

The best vessels for canning jellies and the like are glass Mason-type jars. Jars and screw bands may be reused as long as they are intact and not rusty; lids may not be reused, but they are easily purchased by themselves. Jars should be thoroughly washed and rinsed, then placed, facing up, in a boiling water canner (a large pot with a rack for the jars). Fill the canner with hot water to an inch above the jars' tops, cover the canner, and bring the water to a boil. Simmer for ten minutes.

Clean screw bands should be heated in hot water in a separate saucepan until they come to a boil. For convenience, I like to place my ladle and tongs in this saucepan as well to help them stay as sterile as they can for use in placing my jellies in jars. The jar lids should not be boiled, but they may be warmed gently in a small saucepan of water so that they are near the temperature of the jars and screw bands. When heating the lids, be sure to place them in the pan facing in alternate directions (that is, the first lid faces up, the second one down, and so on) to prevent their sticking together.

When you are ready to place your jelly (or jam or whatever) in its jar, carefully remove the sterilized jars from their hot bath with tongs, and place the jars on your counter on a towel to protect both the jars and the counter. (Re-cover the canner and leave it on low heat so that the water in it is almost boiling.) Gently ladle the jelly into the jars (a clean canning funnel is helpful), leaving about 1/2 inch of headspace at the top of the jars. With a clean, damp paper towel, wipe off the jar rims. Carefully place a lid on each jar with your tongs, and gently screw it on with a screw band. Turn off the heat in the bath, and return the jars to it. Then bring it gently to a boil, and simmer the jars the requisite amount of time.

Once you have finished processing, return the jars to the towel-covered counter, cover them with another towel, and leave them overnight to cool. Test the seals the following day to make sure that the jars have worked their magic. (If you hear a series of "pings" soon after you remove the jars from the bath, you will know that the magic is taking hold.) Store the jars in a cool, dark place until you are ready to use them.

Basil or Rosemary Jelly

I have tried a number of herbal jellies, and I find these two the most flavorful and attractive. For the basil jelly, use a combination of green and purple basil. The jelly's exact color depends on the proportion of purple basil used. It can vary from a pale rose to a deep amethyst. The orange juice in the rosemary jelly loses its flavor in the cooking as it is overpowered by the rosemary. It gives the jelly a gorgeous tint, however. Basil jelly is tasty with almost any meat, especially a pot roast. Rosemary jelly works well with chicken or lamb.

2 cups liquid (water for basil jelly, orange juice for rosemary)
1 cup fresh basil or rosemary leaves, packed
3-1/2 cups sugar
1 tablespoon lemon juice
a dab of sweet butter
1 pouch (3 ounces) liquid pectin

Place the water or juice and the herbs in a covered non-aluminum saucepan. Heat them just to the boiling point; then turn off the heat and let the mixture sit, covered, for at least 20 minutes. Strain the liquid through cheesecloth and discard the herbs.

Return the herbal liquid to the saucepan, and add the sugar, lemon juice, and butter. Do not cover. Bring the mixture to a full, rolling boil, stirring frequently. Add the pectin and return to full boil. Boil for 1 minute, stirring constantly. Remove from heat and skim off any foam. Pour into sterilized jars and process for 5 minutes. (See "About Processing," page 123.)

Makes 4 to 5 cups.

Berry Vinegar

My friend Bobbie is always trying new commercial raspberry vinegars, but she tells me that this Shaker-based recipe is still the best she has ever tasted. The secret: LOTS of berries—and the sugar, which preserves the full fruit flavor. The strawberry or raspberry vinegar may be used in a fairly complex vinaigrette (such as the Merry Lion Sweet and Sour formula on page 127) or simply mixed with good extra-virgin olive oil (two portions of oil to one of vinegar) for a plain but refreshing salad dressing. A dollop of the blueberry vinegar enhances the flavor of a fruit salad. I haven't specified a yield because the proportion of liquid you get from this recipe depends upon the juiciness of the berries you use. Don't try to make a large quantity at a time, or you'll go crazy waiting for your sugar syrup to boil; start with a quart or two of berries.

strawberries, raspberries, or blueberries
enough distilled white vinegar to cover them
equal amounts of sugar and water

Place the berries in a non-aluminum pan (I use a porcelain casserole dish). Cover them with the vinegar, and leave them to soak, covered, overnight. If you forget them for a day and wait 2 nights, they will still be fine.

The next day (or the day after that), gently strain the juice through cheesecloth. You may squeeze the berries a little, but don't overdo; letting the juice drip out on its own is best. Measure the juice. Then measure a little under 1-1/2 times as much sugar and water as juice into a saucepan (i.e., if you have a cup of juice, use just under 1-1/2 cups of sugar and 1-1/2 cups of water). Cook the sugar/water mixture until it threads. Measure the resultant sugar syrup. Add an equal quantity of berry juice to it, and boil the mixture for 10 minutes.

Strain this boiled vinegar through cheesecloth, and decant it into sterilized bottles. Cork or cover. Stored in the dark, berry vinegar should keep its color and flavor for up to a year.

Herbal Vinegar

You may prepare many herb vinegars this way–tarragon and dill are my favorites (dill is great mixed with garlic OR with garlic and peppercorns!)–but I've written this recipe down with basil, which produces a gorgeous color.

1 quart distilled white vinegar
1/2 cup basil leaves, mixed green and purple

Heat the vinegar in a non-aluminum pan until it is just about to boil but not boiling. While it is heating, wash and dry the basil leaves, being careful not to crush them. Gently push the leaves into a warm, clean glass jar with a capacity greater than a quart. (I use an old liquor bottle–washed, of course.)

When the vinegar is warm, pour it into the jar and close the jar loosely. Tighten the jar lid after the vinegar cools. Place the jar in a cool, dry place for 3 days, gently shaking it twice a day. Do NOT try to shake the bottle just after you pour in the hot vinegar as it may leak or explode.

Strain the vinegar and bottle it in smaller bottles. You may seal them if you wish, but you don't have to; vinegar lasts for months and months unsealed. Makes 1 quart.

Mint Syrup

This syrup adds zing to punch or to hot or cold tea. If you store it for more than a couple of months, you may have to thin it out by heating it with additional water. Make sure it is either well sealed or refrigerated, or it will mold .

8 sprigs fresh spearmint
8 sprigs fresh peppermint
(If you don't have both, use twice as much of either.)
2-1/2 cups sugar
1 cup water
1 or 2 drops of green food coloring (optional)

Wash and the mints and blot them dry. Place them in a saucepan, and pound or crush them slightly to release their flavors. Add the sugar and water, and bring the mixture to a boil, stirring until the sugar dissolves. Turn down the heat, and simmer for 15 minutes. Stir in the food coloring, if desired, and remove from heat. Let cool for a few minutes, and strain through cheesecloth into a sterilized jar or bottle. Makes about 2 cups.

Merry Lion Sweet-and-Sour Vinaigrette

This salad dressing makes use of both the berry and the herbal vinegars. Its name comes from that of my mother's former antique shop (and my sales center), the Merry Lion.

1 teaspoon Dijon mustard
2 cloves garlic, crushed
2 tablespoons herbal vinegar
2 tablespoons berry vinegar
1 tablespoon water
2 tablespoons fresh salad herbs (oregano, dill, parsley, basil)
ground pepper to taste
a pinch of salt
9 tablespoons olive or canola oil (or a mixture)

Combine all the ingredients except the oil in a jar. Shake to mix; then add the oil and shake again well. Test with the "finger" method; only your finger can tell you whether the mixture is just right for you. Adjust the flavors to taste. Store the vinaigrette in the refrigerator, and it will last for at least a week. Be sure to shake it again just before you toss the mixture onto salads.

Serves 12.

Chicken with Raspberry Vinegar

This recipe is based on one invented by Leslie Cooper, whose home near Pudding Hollow is known as Strawberry Hill. You may perform all stages up to the addition of the sour cream in advance.

1 chicken (about 2-1/2 pounds), cut into 8 pieces
salt and pepper to taste
sweet butter and extra-virgin olive oil as needed for frying, plus a bit more butter
15 baby carrots (more or less), chopped small
1 large onion, finely chopped
2 cloves garlic, minced
1/3 cup raspberry vinegar
1 bay leaf
about 1/2 cup beef stock
about 2 cups chicken stock
1 cup sour cream
chopped parsley

Season the chicken with the salt and pepper, and brown the pieces lightly in butter and oil. Place them on a dish, and set aside. Pour off the fat from the skillet, and add a bit more butter. Sauté the vegetables until they are wilted. Stir in the vinegar and bay leaf. Return the chicken to the skillet, and add stock almost to cover the pieces. Simmer the chicken pieces until they are soft and the stock is reduced (about 1/2 hour). Remove the chicken again, and place it on a warm serving dish. Add the sour cream to the sauce in the skillet, and cook over high heat until thickened. Pour this sauce over the chicken, and garnish with the parsley. Serve with noodles and a salad tossed with raspberry vinaigrette.

Serves 4 to 5.

Liza's Mustard

Liza Pyle of Singing Brook Farm inherited this recipe from her grandmother. It is Liza's staple holiday gift. In late November she routinely buys several 16-ounce cans of dry mustard to transform into this hot, flavorful spread.

4 ounces (about 1-1/4 cups) dry mustard
(Liza prefers Colman's)
1 cup herbal vinegar (Liza uses tarragon;
dill-garlic is also delicious)
1/4 pound (1 stick) sweet butter, cut into chunks
3/4 cup sugar
1 teaspoon salt
6 eggs

Place the mustard in a small non-aluminum mixing bowl, and pour the vinegar over it. Do not blend the two at this stage. Cover the mixture, and let it stand overnight.

Have the butter cut and the sugar and salt measured so that they can be grabbed quickly when they are needed. Place the mustard mixture in the top of a double boiler, and mix it with a wire whisk over hot water. Add the eggs one at a time, whisking continuously until they are thoroughly mixed.

Add the butter, sugar, and salt, and cook over hot water for 5 minutes, whisking. Liza warns against overcooking as the eggs may curdle. It's better to have slightly runny mustard (it will thicken as it cools anyway) than to risk this.

Ladle the mustard into hot, clean jars. Cool them slightly, then cover and refrigerate them. The mustard will take a couple of weeks to develop its full flavor and will keep for months thereafter in the refrigerator. Makes 3 to 4 cups.

Aunt Lura's Cranberry Chutney

This delightful side spread is more a conserve than a chutney; it is sweet and fruity rather than spicy. My mother's sister makes welcome gifts of it every year at holiday time.

1/4 cup orange juice
4 cups fresh cranberries
1 peeled, seeded orange, cut in chunks
2 cups sugar
1 cup peeled, cored, and chopped apple
1/2 cup raisins
1/2 cup walnuts, chopped
1 tablespoon cider vinegar
1/2 teaspoon ground ginger
1/2 teaspoon cinnamon

Place all the ingredients in a pan and cook until tender. Ladle into sterilized jars and process in a boiling-water bath for 10 minutes. (See "About Processing," page 123.) Makes about 5 cups.

Horseradish Jelly

The jelly is delicious with pot roast or any other dish with which you would eat horseradish; its sweet yet pungent taste really brings out other flavors. And its vibrant color makes it a terrific gift.

1 jar (6 ounces) prepared red horseradish
cider vinegar as needed
3-1/2 cups sugar
a dab of sweet butter
1 pouch (3 ounces) liquid pectin

Place the horseradish in a liquid measuring cup, and add enough vinegar to measure 1-3/4 cups. Pour the liquid into a saucepan. Stir in the sugar and butter, and cook until the mixture comes to a full boil, stirring constantly. Stir in the pectin. Return to a rolling boil, and boil for 1/2 minute, stirring constantly. Remove from heat and stir for 5 minutes to distribute the horseradish evenly through the jelly. Ladle into sterilized jars, and process in a boiling-water bath for 5 minutes. (See "About Processing," page 123.) Makes about 4 cups.

The Peaceable Kingdom

Judy & The Peaceable Kingdom

This cookbook would not be complete without a series of recipes in remembrance of the person who provided its name and its art, Judith Russell. Recipes may seem an odd way of paying tribute to someone's memory. I find that cooking and eating are wonderful ways of bringing people to mind, however. They add a sensory, concrete experience to the act of remembering.

Judy didn't like talking about her past, so I don't know much about her life before she moved into my mother's antique shop, the Merry Lion, in the mid-1980s. I know that she had been married twice, and that she had three children of whom she was very fond but from whom she was independent. I also know that she had taught school for many years, sharing her artistic talents with elementary-school pupils, many of whom visited her years later with happy memories.

A few years before we met, Judy had decided to give up teaching and earn her living entirely as an artist–not an easy decision for anyone, especially someone of middle age. Her paintings were gorgeous, but they took a long time to complete, and sometimes an even longer time to sell, so money was scarce. She became expert at preparing inexpensive meals, finding clothing at thrift shops, and making do with whatever accommodations came along.

Her home in Shelburne, which she and her son Wes had built, was dubbed the Frogcastle after one of her fantasy creations. It had only wood heat and was hard to get in and out of in snowy weather, so she started spending winters in my mother's shop in Shelburne Falls. Eventually, she sold the house as it was too hard to maintain financially, and she spent the remaining years of her life in and out of the Merry Lion.

She became a familiar figure in Shelburne Falls, sitting at her charming painted desk (built by Wes and decorated by Judy) and chatting to customers. She always pictured herself as shy, but she had a remarkable knack for getting to know a great deal about people, and for making her presence felt. She and my mother made a terrific team in the shop, complementing each other's interpersonal skills and sharing a sense of humor.

Judy was 60 when she died in 1994, but somewhere in the course of her life she developed an ageless quality. Children adored her; she never lost her spirit of play or her delight in toys. She loved to construct miniature people and furniture out of whatever materials she had at hand, and the world was her coloring book.

Judy viewed life through rose-colored eyes (even the photographs she took always had a slightly rosy hue), and she refused to look at or think about anything bad. This trait occasionally maddened those of us who loved her; she always retreated from conflict instead of fighting and never really learned how to deal with anything upsetting. Nevertheless, it endeared her to us as well.

One of her favorite painting motifs reflects this positive view of the world. Time and time again, she painted the scene of the Peaceable

Kingdom–lions lying down with lambs and other animals, often in scenes of the local countryside. Judy truly seemed to believe in a world in which diverse creatures and people frolicked and rested together. She made those around her believe in it a bit, too.

Her friend Joanne McMullin suggested after Judy's death that in a way Judy herself constructed a sort of peaceable kingdom around her, bringing together people of varying backgrounds and temperaments who might otherwise never have been friends. In that sense she left us gifts that went way beyond her art.

Her culinary tastes, too, created a peaceable kingdom. She wasn't strong on nutritional planning. Instead, she enjoyed sampling a bit of this and that, and she dipped heavily into carbohydrates. Comfort food was her mainstay; her ideal meal consisted of turkey, mashed potatoes, and gravy, and she was a sucker for a good potato chip.

In general, Judy wasn't much of a cook herself, which made her even more appreciative of the cooking skills of others. She always said that she and I made a great culinary team–and, as you will see, we did team up in cooking as well as in writing. Foods she created looked great but had little taste, and foods I created looked a bit peculiar but tasted wonderful. Together, we had fun cooking and eating–and planning this book.

Jam Dandy

The first two recipes in this chapter originated with Judy herself. Her friend Bernice Arms provided the formula for this cake-like dessert, which Bernice says she was served once by Judy and adopted for her own use. It may be eaten with whipped cream or ice cream–or by itself.

3/4 cup milk
1 egg
1-1/2 cups flour
1/4 cup sugar
2-1/2 teaspoons baking powder
1/4 cup shortening
1/4 cup brown sugar, firmly packed
1/4 cup chopped nuts
2/3 cup jam (any flavor; I prefer strawberry-rhubarb)

Preheat the oven to 375 degrees. Combine the milk and egg. Add the next 4 ingredients, and beat for 50 quick strokes with a fork. Place the dough in a greased, 9-inch-square pan. Sprinkle the top with the brown sugar and nuts. Dot with jam. Bake for 25 to 30 minutes, and serve warm.

Serves 9.

Judy's Pumpkin Bread

Here's another recipe from Judy, given to me by her friend, artist Carolyn Carter. Carolyn says, "Many moons ago when Judy was a teacher in Paxton (Massachusetts), she invited me to lunch and made this delicious pumpkin bread. Ever since then it has been a tradition in my family to harvest a pumpkin from the patch and make these breads in cans as suggested or in small tins to help Santa with stockings or give as gifts. Whatever the reason, every time I make the breads, I think of Judy and our time together." The recipe can be halved if you want to try just a bit of it. If you make your own pumpkin puree instead of obtaining it from a can, be sure to reserve the liquid the pumpkin generates to use instead of water.

2-2/3 cups sugar (Carolyn says this may be varied according to taste.)
2/3 cup canola oil
1-1/2 cups pumpkin puree
4 large eggs
3-1/3 cups flour
1/2 teaspoon baking powder
2 teaspoons baking soda
1-1/2 teaspoons salt
1/2 teaspoon cinnamon (I use a bit more)
1 cup chopped nuts
1 pound chopped dates
2/3 cup water or pumpkin water

Preheat the oven to 300 degrees. Blend the sugar, oil, and pumpkin. Add the eggs to the mixture 1 at a time, beating after each addition. Sift the flour. Then mix together the flour, baking powder, baking soda, salt, and cinnamon.

Dredge the nuts and dates in the dry ingredients. Mix together the nuts, dates, flour mixture, and pumpkin mixture. Add the water and mix well.

Pour into 4 washed and greased 1-pound coffee cans (actually, these days they're as small as 11 ounces) until the cans are half full. Bake in uncovered cans for 60 to 75 minutes, until a toothpick inserted into the bread comes out clean.

Allow the bread to cool, loosen it from the cans, and serve. To store it, put it back in the cans and replace the plastic lids.

Makes 4 loaves.

Cousin Nancy's Chicken Soup

The next few recipes are for foods Judy loved but didn't necessarily make herself. This extra-strong chicken soup comes from Judy's cousin, Nancy Price, who lived in California but flew east to visit Judy regularly. It was a dish Judy especially wanted to include in the cookbook.

1 whole chicken
6 cloves garlic
1 cup each chopped celery, onions, and carrots
3 to 4 chicken bouillon cubes
1 lemon (in slices or just its juice)
salt and pepper to taste
rice, potatoes, or noodles to taste
other vegetables, if desired, to taste
spices/herbs to taste

Boil the chicken, garlic, vegetables, bouillon cubes, lemon, and salt and pepper in a large pot of water until the chicken falls apart. Remove the chicken and lemon (if using the slices) from the broth. Discard the lemon. When the chicken is cool, bone it and set the meat aside. Puree the broth in a blender or food processor. Place it in the refrigerator and let it cool until the fat comes to the top and solidifies. Skim off fat.

Replace the chicken in the stock, and add rice, potatoes, or noodles as well as any vegetables that suit your fancy. Nancy put in carrots, green beans, zucchini–whatever she had at hand. "Use your imagination," she said. Add curry powder, parsley, rosemary, thyme, and/or any combination of spices you desire. Heat thoroughly.

Makes 4 quarts or more, depending on how much you add. Nancy liked to make a pot and eat it all week.

Hamburger Stroganoff

Judy was always happy to eat this inexpensive but delicious version of Beef Stroganoff.

1 cup minced onion
1 clove minced garlic
a dab of sweet butter
1 pound ground beef
1/4 pound mushrooms, sliced and sautéed in sweet butter
1 can (6 ounces) pitted ripe olives
1 chicken bouillon cube
water as needed
salt and pepper to taste
1 cup sour cream, or enough to cover the mixture
a sprinkle of fresh or dried dill

Sauté the onion and garlic in the butter. Stir in the beef and brown it. Drain off the fat if it looks excessive. Add the mushrooms, olives, and bouillon cube, plus enough water to cover the mixture and salt and pepper to taste.

Partially cover and cook for 20 minutes to half an hour, until the liquid has almost evaporated. Stir in the sour cream and heat but do not boil. Sprinkle dill over the Stroganoff and serve over rice or noodles.

Serves 4.

Corn Casserole

Here's another comfort-food recipe Judy loved. I learned to make it from my friend and roommate Kelly King Boyd during my days as a graduate student in Tennessee. It can be as hot or as mild as you want, depending on the number of hot peppers you add.

2 eggs
2 tablespoons flour
salt and pepper to taste
1 green or red bell pepper, diced
fresh or pickled hot peppers, to taste (optional)
1/2 of a 4-ounce jar of pimentos, drained and diced
1/4 pound Cheddar cheese, grated
2 tablespoons melted sweet butter
1 can (15-1/4 ounces) whole kernel corn

Preheat the oven to 350 degrees. Beat the eggs. Stir in the flour, salt and pepper, peppers, pimentos, cheese, and butter. Add the corn with its liquid, and stir.

Bake in a 1-1/2-quart casserole dish for 45 minutes.

Serves 4.

Aunt Lena's Bread-and-Butter Pickles

Judy never said no to a jar of pickles–and bread-and-butter pickles were a particular favorite. She was thrilled when this recipe was submitted for the cookbook and couldn't wait to sample it. Aunt Lena's recipe comes from Lena's niece, Alice H. Godfrey of Buckland. Alice explains, "Lena LaBelle Hartwell grew up on what is called LaBelle Road in Hawley. Her father bought the house on old Cooley Brook Farm Road in the late 1890s. It was the first house on that road at that time. The Cooley family used to come up for picnics at the LaBelles' each summer years ago." Lena LaBelle Hartwell turned 100 in 2003!

6 small unpeeled cucumbers, thinly sliced
6 small onions, thinly sliced
1/3 cup Kosher salt
10 to 12 ice cubes
4 cups sugar
1-1/2 teaspoons turmeric
1-1/2 teaspoons celery seed
2 tablespoons mustard seed
3 cups cider or white vinegar

Combine the cucumbers, onions, and salt. Add the ice cubes and let stand for 3 hours. Drain well. Place the vegetables and the remaining ingredients in a large, non-aluminum pot, and bring the mixture to a boil.

Ladle into sterilized jars, and seal at once. If you wish to be extra careful, process for 10 minutes. (See "About Processing," page 123.)

Makes 3 pints.

Dragon Brook Farm Peach-Ginger Chutney

Judy was eager to include this recipe in our book. It comes from Mary "Mitzi" Torras, a strong supporter of the efforts of the Franklin Land Trust, who lives on a Shelburne property known as Dragon Brook Farm. Feel free to experiment with the ginger by adding 2 ounces, then tasting and adding more if needed. The full 6 ounces will make a fairly hot chutney. Mitzi doesn't process her jars, but I always feel a bit more secure doing so.

2 pounds (about 4-1/2 cups) sugar
1 quart cider vinegar
4 pounds very ripe peaches, peeled, cored, and cut up (about 8 cups of peach pieces)
1-1/2 cups raisins (yellow raisins are attractive)
2 tablespoons mustard seed
1 tablespoon crushed red pepper
1 clove garlic, minced
2 to 6 ounces crystallized ginger, chopped into small pieces

Combine the sugar and vinegar. Boil them uncovered, stirring frequently, until they form a thick syrup. (This will take about 1 hour.) Add the peaches, raisins, mustard seed, pepper, and garlic. Boil again until the mixture is very thick, about 30 minutes longer.

Add the ginger and cook for ten minutes longer. Ladle the chutney into sterilized jars. Process the jars for 10 minutes. (See "About Processing," page 123.) Makes 4 to 5 pints.

Crystallized Violets and Johnny Jump-Ups

This is one recipe Judy made a lot better than I ever could! Judy, who adored all flowers, created candied violets, johnny jump-ups, and even miniature roses. You might want to try any of these, plus lilac blossoms, pansies, carnations, or borage. The most important thing about this procedure is keeping a light hand.

edible flowers
egg white
superfine sugar

Pick the flowers when they are fresh and dry. Place their stems in water until you are ready to use them. Then pluck the flowers from the stems.

Whip the egg white slightly with a fork. Then take a very thin, small paint brush and daintily cover the flower with the white. Gently move the flower through the superfine sugar–or sprinkle it on gingerly with your fingers. Put the flower on wax paper, and allow it to dry and harden. (This will take several hours.) Place the finished flowers in an air-tight container. They will last for months.

Froggie Chocolate Cake

At one time, Judy and I thought about becoming professional bakers. I would bake cakes, we thought, and she would decorate them. Our baking association lasted as long as it took us to make the first cake, when we realized that we would NEVER make enough money to compensate us for our time. Even so, we enjoyed the experience. A friend requested a chocolate cake for her son, who was crazy about monsters. I used the cake and icing recipes below, which came from Mary Parker. When the cake was complete, Judy created a shiny lake on top of it (by dying superfine sugar greenish blue with food coloring), stuck in a few "water lilies" of candied edible flowers (see previous page), and stuck plastic frogs from the dime store around her lake's perimeter. The cake made a big hit—but Judy and I retired anyway.

1/2 cup (1 stick) sweet butter, at room temperature
1-1/2 cups sugar
2 eggs
2 squares (1 ounce each) baking chocolate
3/4 cup hot water
2 cups flour
2 teaspoons baking powder
1 teaspoon baking soda
1/2 cup milk

Preheat the oven to 350 degrees. Cream together the butter and the sugar. Add the eggs, 1 at a time. Melt the chocolate in the hot water. Sift together the dry ingredients, and add them to the butter mixture alternately with the milk. Stir in the chocolate and hot water. Pour into 2 greased and floured 8-inch layer pans, and bake for 25 to 30 minutes.

Makes a 2-layer cake.

Ice with Great-Grandmother Schneider's Chocolate Frosting.

Great Grandmother Schneider's Chocolate Frosting

This is the favorite frosting of Mary Parker's daughter Alice. Alice likens it to "pouring fudge over your cake."

2 cups sugar
4 squares (1 ounce each) baking chocolate
2 eggs
6 tablespoons milk
2 teaspoons vanilla

Place the sugar, chocolate, eggs, and milk in a saucepan. Bring the mixture to a boil, and boil for 3 minutes, stirring constantly. Remove the pan from the heat, and stir in the vanilla. Cool the mixture slightly, and spread it carefully on the cake.

Asparagus à la Bambi

Judy's friend Bambi Miller is an enthusiastic gardener who shared Judy's love of frogs and of play. The librarian in Charlemont, Bambi perpetuates Judy's memory by leading a yearly workshop for kids that explores some aspect of the world through Judy's imaginary creation, the Frogcastle.

1 pound fresh asparagus
extra-virgin olive oil as needed
LOTS of garlic–about 5 cloves, chopped
fresh basil or cilantro (optional), chopped
1/4 pound feta cheese
freshly ground pepper

Blanch or steam the asparagus for 1 minute in its own pan, and remove it quickly. Coat a frying pan with oil and then add another big splash. Heat the oil to high but do not burn it. Sizzle the garlic in the olive oil, tossing in the basil or cilantro, if desired.

Add the asparagus and quickly sear. Remove it from the pan. Place the asparagus on a serving dish. Put the cooked garlic on top, and crumble feta cheese on top of that. Drizzle the remaining oil from the pan onto the cheese. Grind fresh pepper over all.

This dish may be served hot or cold. Serves 2 as a main dish or 4 as a side dish. Bambi insists that the asparagus must be eaten with one's fingers.

Self-Portrait: Granny Toad

My Squash Pie

Humble Pie

In November, hilltown dwellers suddenly observe the onset of winter and sigh a bit. Grey and nippy day succeeds grey and nippy day. The foliage has fallen off the trees and remains only a memory. We need warmth and solace. On such days no food is so gratifying to bake and serve as a hearty pie.

Pie is a grand old Yankee tradition that brings out the whimsy in many of our countrymen and women. Humorist and philosopher Don Marquis once quipped, "I love you as New Englanders love pie!" And Harriet Beecher Stowe wrote in *Oldtown Folks,* "The pie is an English institution, which, planted on American soil, forthwith ran rampant and burst forth into an untold variety of genera and species."

My favorite writer on cold weather and pie is Charles Dudley Warner (1829-1900). Warner, the man of letters who co-wrote *The Gilded Age* with Mark Twain, spent his childhood not far from Pudding Hollow, in one of the oldest houses in Charlemont. Warner penned a series of humorous essays called "Backlog Studies" that echo many of my own feelings about the need to snuggle indoors on a gray day.

"I have never sat upon a throne,—except in moments of a traveler's curiosity, about as long as a South American dictator remains on one," reflected Warner, "but I have no idea that it compares, for pleasantness, with a seat before a wood-fire…. The fireplace … is a window through which we look out upon other scenes."

In the midst of his fireside musings, Warner speculated about a possible "diet line" stretching from east to west across the center of New England, demarcating what he termed the region of perpetual pie. "In this region," he suggested, "pie is to be found at all hours and seasons, and at every meal."

"I am not sure, however," Warner went on, "that pie is not a matter of altitude rather than latitude, as I find that all the hill and country towns of New England are full of those excellent women, the very salt of the housekeeping earth, who would feel ready to sink in mortification through their scoured kitchen floors, if visitors should catch them without a pie in the house."

"The absence of pie," he concluded with tongue in cheek, "would be more noticed than a scarcity of Bible even."

I may not scour my floor quite so frequently as those dames of yore whom Warner conjured up. In fact, I'm more the pepper than the salt of the housekeeping earth. Nevertheless, I do love to serve pies to my friends and neighbors in the chilly countryside as we bask beside the fire. This ultimate comfort food warms the house through baking, the body through eating, and the heart through sharing.

The pie recipes I present here are easy to prepare and satisfying to eat. True to Warner's notion of "perpetual pie," they can be eaten for lunch and even (well, most of them) for breakfast as well as for dinner. They gladden the gloomiest of days.

Keenan Cuisine Chicken Pot Pie

Philip Keenan and Jane O'Connor are a husband-wife cooking team, the former owners of a catering service called Keenan Cuisine in Hawley. Phil was kind enough to share this recipe with me. Note: I'm not the world's most successful pastry chef, and I have a bit of trouble rolling out Phil's extra-rich crusts. You may use a more basic recipe—such as the one on page 147—but if you have any pastry skills, do try this one.

for the stock:
the carcass of 1 chicken
onion skins, coarsely chopped
celery tops, coarsely chopped
parsley stems, coarsely chopped
carrot heads, coarsely chopped
5 cups cold water

for the pie dough (2 2-crust pies):
2-1/2 cups sweet butter, lard, or shortening
3-3/4 cups flour
1-1/4 cups water

for the pie filling:
1/3 to 1/2 cup peeled carrots, diced or cubed
3 medium peeled potatoes, diced coarsely
(1 to 1-1/2 cups chopped)
1 quart of the chicken stock
4 6-ounce boneless breasts of chicken,
cut into 1-inch cubes
(or 1-1/2 pounds chicken meat pulled from the
bone; use the carcass for stock)
1/2 cup (1 stick) sweet butter
1 small to medium onion, coarsely chopped
(1/3 to 1/2 cup chopped)
1/3 to 1/2 cup coarsely chopped celery
3/4 cup flour
salt and pepper to taste
sage and thyme to taste (optional)

To prepare the stock: Place all the ingredients in a pot and simmer for an hour and a half. Strain through a sieve.

To prepare the crust: Cut the fat into the flour until you have marble-sized lumps; then stir in the water little by little with a fork, and refrigerate for an hour. Roll out into 4 (2 top and 2 bottom) 9-inch crusts.

To prepare the filling: Blanch the carrots and potatoes in the stock. Sauté the chicken in half of the butter in a large skillet until browned. Remove the chicken from the skillet and toss in the remaining butter, the onion, and the celery. Sauté until the onion pieces become opaque. Add the flour and continue to cook, stirring, until the flour begins to turn golden (5 to 10 minutes). Then add the stock and the blanched carrots and potatoes to the pot, and stir while the mixture thickens. Add the chicken once more. Finish by adding salt and pepper to taste, along with sage and thyme if desired.

The filling may be cooled and placed in 2 unbaked pastry shells with tops, then baked in a 350-degree oven until the crusts are browned and the pot pie bubbles through slits made on top (45 minutes to 1 hour). If desired, the filling may also be heated and served on egg noodles or rice without the pie crust. Serves 8 to 10.

Shepherd's Pie

This traditional dish isn't actually a pie; that is, it doesn't have a pastry crust. Nevertheless, its potato topping is close to a crust, and its hearty warmth is pie-like.

2 tablespoons sweet butter
2 cups cubed cooked lamb or beef
1 large onion, finely chopped–
or a leek, sliced thinly
1 stalk celery, chopped
1 clove garlic, finely chopped
1 regular carrot or several baby carrots, sliced
2 tablespoons flour
1/2 cup beef broth
2 teaspoons Worcestershire sauce, more or less
1 can (11 to 15-1/4 ounces) whole kernel corn, drained, or 2 cups fresh corn kernels
salt and pepper to taste
1 teaspoon dried rosemary (for lamb)
or
2 tablespoons chopped fresh parsley (for beef)
2 cups hot, mashed potatoes (about three potatoes)
grated Cheddar cheese (optional)

Preheat the oven to 450 degrees. In a 10-inch skillet over medium heat in hot butter, cook the lamb (or beef), onion, celery, garlic, and carrots until the onion and celery are tender, stirring often. Stir in the flour, and gradually add the beef broth. Cook until the mixture boils, stirring constantly. Stir in the Worcestershire, corn, salt, pepper, and spices. Turn the meat mixture into an 8-by-8-inch baking dish. Spread the potatoes over the mixture, and grate cheese over the top if desired.

Bake for 20 minutes or until the potatoes are lightly browned. Serves 4.

Note: If you have no leftover lamb or beef, you may use 1 pound ground raw lamb or beef. Omit the butter and increase the broth to 1 cup. Drain off the fat after cooking the meat with the vegetables.

Canadian Shepherd's Pie

This succulent meat pie comes from Denis Carrier, a native of Quebec who visits neighbors of mine regularly. Denis informs me that the recipe actually comes from his mother, Renée Rhéaume. As far as I'm concerned, they're both great cooks. Note: You may halve the recipe and make only 1 pie. If so, you will definitely want to follow Denis's advice and add more wine.

2 whole chicken breasts, boned, skinned, and diced
sweet butter and oil as needed for sautéing
1/2 cup white wine (actually, Denis uses even more to keep everything moist)
1 medium onion or its equivalent in scallions, chopped
1 can (10 ounces) mushrooms, drained, or
1 cup sautéed fresh mushrooms
1-1/4 cups beef broth
1 tablespoon cornstarch
1-1/2 pounds ground pork
parsley, salt, pepper, and savory to taste
2 double 9-inch pie crusts

Cook the chicken pieces in oil and butter until brown. Remove the chicken from the frying pan. Deglaze the fat with 1/4 cup of the wine. Pour the resulting sauce over the chicken in a bowl.

Place more oil and butter in the frying pan and brown the onions and mushrooms. Again remove the contents of the pan, and deglaze with 1/4 cup wine.

Add the broth to the sauce in the pan. Make the cornstarch into a paste with a small amount of water, then add it to the broth and boil until thick, stirring frequently.

Add the pork. Simmer for 20 minutes on low heat. Then add the seasonings, vegetables, and chicken. Place the mixture in the 2 bottom pie crusts and cover with the top crusts. Poke holes in the top of the pies for ventilation.

Bake at 425 degrees for 30 minutes, or until the pie is done.

Serves 8 to 12.

Tamale Pie

This recipe, from an old friend of my parents, resembles a shepherd's pie.

1 large onion, finely chopped
1 green pepper, finely chopped
1 large clove garlic, pressed or minced
canola oil as needed for sautéing
1 pound hamburger, broken up
1/2 pound bulk breakfast sausage, broken up
1 bottle (5-3/4 ounces) stuffed green olives, chopped
2 cups canned or stewed tomatoes
1 bay leaf
salt and pepper to taste
1 teaspoon chili powder (or a bit more)
a dash of nutmeg
1/2 cup plus sharp Cheddar cheese, grated
1/2 cup cornmeal
2 cups cold water
1/2 teaspoon salt

In a medium saucepan, sauté the onion, green pepper, and garlic in oil. Add the hamburger and sausage, and cook until brown. Drain the fat if you have a lot. Stir in the olives (save a few for garnish), tomatoes, and spices. Simmer for 2 to 4 hours. Stir in the cheese, reserving some for the top. Preheat the oven to 325 degrees, and make your cornmeal mush. To do this, combine the cornmeal with 1/2 cup of the water. Place the remaining water and the salt in a saucepan, and bring them to a boil. Stir in the cornmeal mixture, and cook, stirring, until the mush is thick. (This takes only a couple of minutes.)

Line a medium casserole dish with the cornmeal mush, then fill with the meat mixture and top with a bit more mush. Decorate with olives and cheese and bake for 1 hour. Serves 6 to 8.

Maple House Pizza Crust

Pizza is, after all, a type of pie. This formula comes from Becky Bradley of Rowe's Maple House bed and breakfast.

3 cups flour
1 package dry yeast
1/2 cup lukewarm water
1/4 cup extra-virgin olive oil
1/2 to 1 cup cold milk

Directions:

Place the flour in a bowl, and make a well in the middle. Dissolve the yeast in the water, and add it to the flour. Stir in the oil and enough milk to make the mixture into a dough.

Let the dough rest for 5 minutes. Turn it onto a floured board. Knead 50 strokes. Let the dough rest for 2 more minutes, and knead another 20 strokes. In an oiled bowl, let the dough rise for 1-1/2 to 2 hours in a warm place. Oil two pizza or jelly-roll pans, divide the dough in two, and stretch each half across a pan. Cover with desired toppings (I like tomato sauce, feta cheese, and black olives), and bake in a preheated 450-degree oven for 15 to 20 minutes, switching oven shelves halfway through. Makes 2 pizza crusts.

Peter's Stilton-Leek Tart

This heavenly pie comes from the fertile culinary imagination of my neighbor Peter Beck.

4 medium leeks
1 tablespoon sweet butter
1 tablespoon extra-virgin olive oil
1 clove garlic, minced
1 wedge Stilton (3 to 4 ounces)
1 9-inch pie shell
4 eggs, beaten
1 pinch nutmeg
1/2 cup light cream
1 tablespoon whisky (or port;
Peter says to "eschew sherry")

Preheat the oven to 375 degrees. Clean the leeks, and remove the root ends and most of the green stalks. Quarter each leek stalk lengthwise, and clean out any remaining soil or sand. Slice across the stalks to form 1/4-inch-wide strips. Sauté the sliced leeks in the butter and oil. Add the garlic and continue to sauté until the leeks have softened a bit (less than 5 minutes). Remove from heat and set aside to cool.

Crumble enough Stilton to yield between 1/2 and 1 full cup of crumbled cheese. Toss the cheese with the leeks, and spoon or pour the mixture into the crust.

Beat the remaining ingredients together until thoroughly combined. Pour them over the leek-and-stilton mixture. With a wooden spoon or spatula, ensure that the mixture and the custard are distributed properly about the crust. Bake the tart for 40 minutes. Remove it when the center is firm, the top has become golden, and the exposed leeks are beginning to brown. Serves 4 as a main course; 8, as an appetizer.

Bob Stone's Fullerville Pie Crust

Bob lives in a section of Hawley known as Fullerville. In early years, Fullerville was a hard, dark place in which to live and farm. It is nestled in a small valley between steep hills, and only a few hours of sunshine touch its lawns and gardens each day. Nevertheless, Fullervillians have always found ways to cheer themselves up. Bob's pie crust rolls out like a dream. The secret, Bob explains, is the vinegar: "No matter how much you work the dough it'll always come out nice and flaky."

4 cups flour
1 teaspoon salt (optional)
1-3/4 cups shortening
1/2 cup cold water plus a bit more if needed
1 tablespoon white vinegar
1 egg

Combine the flour and salt in a bowl. Cut in the shortening, using a pastry blender or two knives, until it is crumbly. Do not overmix. Whisk together the water, vinegar, and egg, and stir them gently into the flour mixture. If the dough seems too dry (this is rare), add a tiny bit more water.

Roll the dough into four circles. Makes enough crust for 2 double 9-inch pies.

Nantucket Cranberry Pie

This recipe from the late Mary Parker is actually a cross between a cookie and a cake, but you make it in a pie pan, so "pie" is just as good a name as any. During the course of cooking, the berries (which start out on the bottom) float toward the top of this dessert, making attractive little bumps. The final product is a tasty combination of sweet and tart.

2 cups raw cranberries
1-1/2 cups sugar
1/2 cup chopped walnuts
3/4 cup (1-1/2 sticks) melted sweet butter
2 eggs, beaten
1 cup flour
1 teaspoon vanilla or almond extract

Grease a 9- or 10-inch pie plate. Preheat the oven to 375 degrees. Wash and pick over the cranberries. Put them in the bottom of the pie plate. Sprinkle with 1/2 cup of the sugar and the walnuts. Make a batter of the remaining ingredients, first combining the butter and the remaining sugar and then adding the eggs, flour, and flavoring. Pour the batter over the cranberries.

Bake for 35 to 40 minutes. Top with whipped cream. (Ice cream works well, too.) Serves 8.

Mock Cherry Pie

Here's another pie that makes use of the cranberry, a fruit we always think of in the late fall. My grandmother loved it and made it regularly. My friend Peter prefers to gussy up its name and call it "Cranberry Cerise."

2 cups cranberries, cut in half
1 cup raisins
1-1/2 cups sugar
1/2 cup water
1 tablespoon flour
1 pinch salt
1 double 8-inch pie crust

Preheat the oven to 425 degrees. Combine the filling ingredients and allow them to sit for a few minutes in a bowl. Place them in the bottom crust, and cover them with another crust or lattice top. Prick holes in the top. Bake for 10 minutes; then reduce the heat to 350 degrees and bake for another 35 to 45 minutes. Serves 6 to 8.

My Grandmother's Squash Pie

Shortly before her marriage, my grandmother studied at the Fannie Farmer Cooking School in Boston. I know Miss Farmer would have approved of this pie, which our family traditionally eats at Thanksgiving.

1-1/2 cups pumpkin or winter squash puree
1/2 cup white sugar
1/2 cup brown sugar, firmly packed
1 teaspoon cinnamon
1/2 teaspoon salt
1/2 teaspoon ginger or allspice (or a bit of each)
1 cup evaporated milk
1/2 cup water
2 eggs
1 9-inch pie shell

Preheat the oven to 425 degrees. Combine the filling ingredients, and place them in the unbaked pie shell. Bake for 10 minutes; then reduce the heat to 350 degrees and bake for another 30 to 40 minutes, or until firm.

Serves 6 to 8.

Apple Pie à la Française

Here's another pie formula from Denis Carrier; my only addition was the salt. This attractive fall pie is like apple crisp in a shell.

3/4 cup sugar
1 teaspoon cinnamon
1 pinch salt
5 medium baking apples, peeled, cored, and sliced
1 9-inch pie shell
1 cup flour
1/2 cup brown sugar, firmly packed
1/2 cup (1 stick) sweet butter

Preheat the oven to 425 degrees. Mix together the sugar, the cinnamon, and the salt. Add them to the apples, and stir gently. Place this mixture in the pie shell. Combine the flour and the brown sugar. Cut in the butter. Cover the apples with this crumb mixture.

Bake for 10 minutes; then reduce the heat to 350 degrees and bake for another half hour, or until the apples are completely cooked. Serves 8.

A Very Short Pie Story

Ernest Kelly of Shelburne told this tale of former Hawley days.

Deacon Harmon thought it was a good thing to teach the kids how to spell so when he passed the dessert around, he asked the kid what he wanted, and the kid had to spell it. And the kid wanted a doughnut.

"Well, spell it."

"No, I'll take pie."

The Pudding Contest

The Pudding Contest

My hometown has an undistinguished history. No one famous was born in Hawley. No great religious or social movement ever took hold here. The town was settled in the 1770s, rather late as Massachusetts communities went, because its rocky soil and hilly terrain rendered agriculture marginal. No record of pre-European inhabitants exists; clearly Native Americans saw that the area was inhospitable long before the first white settlers arrived. No heroes or heroic activities appear in the pages of the town's three (so far) official histories.

Hawley lore recounts one tale that isn't heroic in traditional terms but appeals to me nevertheless, the story of the Pudding Contest. In the town's earliest days, legend has it, two pioneer women took part in the town's first (and, to date, only) bake-off, or rather steam-off. They vied to see who could produce Hawley's largest pudding.

The winner, Abigail Baker, prepared her pudding in a "five-pail kettle," which sounds appropriately vast. She was ever after called Hawley's "Pudding Head," and the area of town in which she lived is known to this day as Pudding Hollow.

The choice of puddings made sense, for puddings dominated 18th-century menus. In an era when fires had to be lit for hours in order to cook properly, slow-cooked foods like puddings proved easy to prepare. According to a delightful 1960 *Gourmet* magazine article titled "Pudding Time," puddings–even sweet ones–were served first in early-American dinners, rather than as after-meal desserts. This practice led to the colloquial expression, "I came in pudding time," meaning, "I came early."

Anglo-Americans prepared traditional English puddings but also adapted themselves to the ingredients at hand, producing Indian puddings and corn puddings as well as plum puddings.

Puddings used available foodstuffs, added nutrition to meals, and filled 18th-century homes like Abigail Baker's with delicious aromas.

Town officials revived the story of the Pudding Contest more than a decade ago for Hawley's bicentennial; its reenactment provided an entertaining scene in the town's celebratory pageant. The scene was treated as comic, and I enjoyed hamming it up as Mrs. Baker, concentrating hard on my cooking and jumping for joy when my pudding was pronounced the winner. Judith Russell's painting of this scene captures the fun of the event.

Despite our emphasis on humor in the pageant, I can't help thinking that the pudding contest was a serious symbolic moment in the town's history. I relate to it particularly because it is the only recorded female act in 18th-century Hawley. Most of the deeds dug up by historians in the town's official records–property purchases, elections of officials, participation in wars–involved only men.

I also love the sheer pragmatism of a contest that forged entertainment out of everyday skills and elevated the preparation of a thick, wholesome substance into a legend. The contest paid tribute to the town's inventiveness, tenacity, and common sense–qualities for Americans to cherish in the 21st century as well as the 18th.

Here I share some New England pudding recipes that might have appealed to Abigail Baker. The time they take in the oven or stove warms the house. And their aromas and flavors bring lively reminders of a tradition that has lasted more than two centuries.

Indian Pudding

As its name suggests, this dish was a gift to New England settlers from Native Americans, a variation on their cornmeal mush. It was probably the most popular pudding in 18th-century America. Like most puddings, it is adaptable; I make it with maple syrup because I like to support local maple farmers, but it is traditionally prepared with molasses. Feel free to omit (or add to) the apples and raisins—and to experiment with spices.

5 cups milk
2/3 cup maple syrup
1/3 cup sugar
1/2 cup yellow cornmeal
1 teaspoon cinnamon
1 teaspoon salt
4 tablespoons sweet butter
2 medium apples
1/2 cup raisins

Heat 4 cups of the milk in a saucepan and add the maple syrup, sugar, cornmeal, cinnamon, salt, and butter. Cook for 20 minutes or until the mixture thickens. Preheat the oven to 300 degrees. Peel and core the apples; then slice them thinly onto the bottom of a medium baking dish. Stir the raisins into the cornmeal mixture, and pour it into the dish on top of the apples. Pour the remaining milk on top, but do not stir it in. Bake for 3 hours without stirring. Serve warm with cream, whipped cream, ice cream, or hard sauce. Serves 8.

Corn Pudding

If you can make this side dish with fresh, raw corn cut off the cob, do so, although canned or frozen corn may be substituted.

2 eggs, slightly beaten
1 tablespoon melted sweet butter
1 cup milk
1 leek, thinly sliced (white part only)
1/2 red bell pepper, diced
1/2 teaspoon salt
freshly ground pepper
2 cups corn kernels

Preheat the oven to 350 degrees. Butter a 1-quart casserole dish. Pour in the eggs; then whisk in the butter, milk, leek, bell pepper, salt, and pepper. Stir in the corn. Place the casserole inside a larger casserole or baking dish on your oven rack. Pour boiling water into the outer pan so that it stands halfway up the side of the inner casserole dish. Bake for about 1 hour—or until a knife inserted an inch from the edge comes out almost clean. Let stand 10 minutes before serving. Serves 4.

Grandmother Parker's Cracker Pudding

This dish is a holiday tradition at Singing Brook Farm in Hawley. (The late Grandmother Parker would now be a great-great-great-great grandmother.) It puffs up into a rich and delicious concoction. The Common Crackers it requires are not actually so very common. If you cannot find them, get in touch with the Vermont Country Store in Weston, Vermont (802-362-8460), and order a package of Vermont Common Crackers.

about 15 New England Common Crackers
softened sweet butter as needed
about 30 seeded muscat raisins
enough milk to cover the crackers and raisins
(about 4 cups)
2 eggs, beaten
1-1/2 to 2 cups sugar
(depending on your sweet tooth)
1/2 teaspoon mace
1/2 teaspoon nutmeg
1 teaspoon salt
1 teaspoon vanilla

Split the crackers in half and spread each half with butter. Put 1 muscat raisin on each half cracker, and arrange the crackers loosely on the bottom of a 3-quart casserole dish. (In my dish, they make 2 layers.)

Cover the crackers with milk and a weighted plate, and allow them to soak overnight in a cool place. (If you're in a hurry, you may use heated milk, which speeds up the process, and allow them to stand for 3 or 4 hours.)

The next day, preheat the oven to 300 degrees. Drain off the milk, and combine it with the remaining ingredients. Cover the crackers with the liquid and bake for 1-1/2 hours. Serve hot with lots and lots of whipped cream. Serves 10.

Asparagus Pudding

This is actually sort of a casserole, but its name demonstrates the flexibility of the word "pudding." It's very fattening and very delicious. My sister-in-law Leigh's family made it for major holidays when she was growing up, and she has brought that tradition to our family. Do not attempt to make it with fresh asparagus; it's one of those rare dishes that actually require canned vegetables.

for the white sauce:
1/4 cup (1/2 stick) sweet butter
1/4 cup flour
1/2 cup asparagus juice drained from cans (see below)
2-1/2 cups milk
freshly ground pepper to taste

for the pudding:
2 cans (15 ounces each) asparagus spears, cut in small pieces; drained but with the juice reserved
3/4 pound Cheddar cheese, grated
1 smallish package slivered almonds (4 to 6 ounces)
1 stack white saltine crackers plus a few more, crushed (about 52 crackers in all)
paprika for color

First, make the white sauce. Over medium heat in a heavy saucepan, melt the butter. Whisk in the flour, and cook for 1 minute, whisking constantly. Gradually stir in the asparagus juice and milk. Continue cooking until the sauce is smooth, thickened, and heated thoroughly, whisking all the time. Grind in the pepper.

Layer the first 4 ingredients of the pudding together in a large casserole dish, saving some almonds and cracker crumbs for the top. Stir the white sauce through the layered dish to mix all ingredients together. Top with the leftover almonds, additional crushed saltines, and paprika. Bake for 30 minutes at 350 degrees, or 60 minutes at 200 degrees; the dish should be heated through. Serves 6 to 8.

Chocolate Pudding

Like many so-called puddings, this is sort of an upside down cake–and it's out of this world, especially if you're a chocolate lover! It thrives on whipped cream.

1-1/4 cups white sugar
1 cup sifted flour
2 teaspoons baking powder
1/3 teaspoon salt
1/2 cup milk
1 teaspoon vanilla
1 square (1 ounce) baking chocolate
2 tablespoons sweet butter
1/2 cup brown sugar, firmly packed
4 tablespoons cocoa
1 cup boiling water

Preheat the oven to 350 degrees. Into a bowl sift 3/4 cup of the sugar with the flour, baking powder, and salt. Beat in the milk and vanilla. Melt the chocolate and butter together in a double boiler. Add them to the other mixture. Pour this batter into a buttered 9-by-9-inch pan. Blend the brown sugar, the remaining white sugar, and the cocoa, and sprinkle them on top of the batter. Pour the water over all. Do not mix it in! Bake for 40 minutes.

Serves 9.

Strawberry Pudding

This tasty pudding (another that resembles an upside-down cake) comes from Denis Carrier. It may be made with half strawberries and half rhubarb.

4 cups fresh strawberries
1-1/2 cups sugar
1-1/3 cups flour
1 tablespoon baking powder
1/2 teaspoon salt
1/4 cup shortening
(Denis uses Crisco; I, sweet butter)
3/4 cup milk
1 egg
1 teaspoon vanilla

Preheat the oven to 350 degrees. Place the fruit in a medium-size casserole dish. Spread 3/4 cup of the sugar over it. In a bowl mix together the flour, remaining sugar, baking powder, and salt. Cut the shortening into the dry ingredients until the mixture becomes crumbly. Beat the milk, egg, and vanilla together. Add the liquid ingredients to the dry ones, and mix just enough to moisten them throughout. Pour this batter over the fruit. Bake for about 45 minutes, until the top of the cake appears light brown and crispy. Serves 6 to 8.

Eric Carle's Bread Pudding

Children's book author and illustrator Eric Carle and his wife Bobby have a home in Hawley. Knowing of my neighbor Florette's passion for puddings, Eric transcribed this recipe for her, and she passed it on to me. I use Grand Marnier for the liqueur. If you want to spoil yourself, top each serving with a bit of heavy cream.

raisins as needed (Eric didn't specify how many; I used 1 cup)

1/2 cup Kirsch, Amaretto, Cointreau, or Grand Marnier

1/4 pound (1 stick) sweet butter

5 cups cubed stale bread; the cubes should be about 1/2-inch in diameter ("French bread, Wonder Bread, old rolls," says Eric. "Not rye bread.")

5 eggs, plus 3 egg yolks

1 cup sugar

1 teaspoon vanilla

1 quart milk

1 quart cream

Preheat the oven to 375 degrees. Butter a 3-quart baking dish. Soften the raisins in hot water for a few minutes; then drain them and soak them in the liqueur. Melt the butter.

Place a layer of bread cubes in the baking dish, followed by a layer of raisins (which you have drained, reserving the liquid) and some melted butter. Repeat this process, making several layers. Pour the leftover liqueur over all.

Whisk together the eggs, egg yolks, sugar, and vanilla.

Combine the milk and cream in a large saucepan, and bring just to the boil, stirring constantly. Remove the saucepan from the heat. Stir a little of this liquid into the egg mixture to warm the eggs gradually so they won't curdle; then add the egg mixture to the milk and cream. Pour this combination over the layered bread crumbs in the baking dish.

Place the baking dish inside a larger dish, and pour boiling water around it. Steam the pudding in the oven for 40 to 45 minutes, until the top bread cubes brown a little. Serves 10 to 12.

Deacon Porter's Hat

This steamed pudding has been served for more than 150 years at my alma mater, Mount Holyoke College. Early students thought it resembled the headgear of Andrew Porter, a supporter of school founder Mary Lyon. (Lyon was born in the West County town of Buckland.) At Mount Holyoke, the pudding is made in a special hat-shaped mold, but any covered mold that holds at least 1-1/2 quarts will do. To purchase a mold, try the King Arthur Flour Baker's Catalogue (800-827-6363) or Williams-Sonoma (800-541-2233). This recipe comes from Dale Hennessey at the college.

1/2 cup raisins
enough orange juice or rum to plump the raisins (optional)
3/4 cup plus 1 tablespoon plus 1 teaspoon buttermilk
1/2 cup molasses
1/2 cup brown sugar, firmly packed
1-3/4 cups flour
1 teaspoon cinnamon
1/8 teaspoon nutmeg
1/8 teaspoon cloves
1/2 teaspoon baking soda
1/4 teaspoon salt
2 tablespoons vegetable shortening
1-1/2 tablespoons sweet butter

Preheat the oven to 350 degrees. If you wish, soak the raisins in orange juice or rum to plump them. Mix together the buttermilk, molasses and brown sugar. In a separate bowl mix together the flour, spices, baking soda and salt. In a small pan over low heat melt together the shortening and butter.

Stir the flour mixture gently into the buttermilk mixture. Stir in the melted shortening and butter mixture. Finally, fold in the raisins, draining them and discarding the liquid if you have plumped them. Grease the pudding mold and its cover. Spoon the batter into the mold. It should fill the mold about 2/3 full. Cover the mold.

Place the mold inside an oven-proof pan, and pour boiling water into the outer pan, enough to reach 1/3 of the way up the side of the mold. Bake the pudding in this water bath in the lower third of the oven for 2-1/2 hours, replacing the water occasionally in the pan as needed so that it maintains its level. Remove the pudding from the oven, invert it on a plate, and let it stand for 20 minutes. Remove the pudding from the mold and let it cool briefly. Wrap in wax paper and refrigerate. Allow the dessert to stand a few days to improve the flavor and texture. To serve, wrap it in foil and reheat gently by steaming it on a rack in a covered pan for about 20 to 30 minutes. Serves 6 to 8.

Hard Sauce for Deacon Porter's Hat

Dale suggests serving Deacon Porter's Hat with a Crème Anglaise, hard sauce, or foamy pudding sauce. My choice is this traditional hard sauce.

1/2 cup (1 stick) sweet butter, at room temperature

2 cups confectioners' sugar

1 teaspoon vanilla or 1 tablespoon rum, according to personal preference

Cream together the butter and sugar. Beat the mixture until it is soft and creamy. Stir in the vanilla or rum, and place the mixture in a bowl.

Cover and refrigerate until needed.

"People Must Have Puddings"

Mary Lyon's best known student, Emily Dickinson, kept her fondness for puddings after she left the Mount Holyoke Female Seminary, as the school was called in its early days.

In 1870 Thomas Wentworth Higginson described a visit to Dickinson's home by writing, "She makes all the bread for her father only likes hers & says '& people must have puddings' this very dreamily, as if they were comets–so she makes them."

Cottage Pudding

Linda Comstock of Charlemont provided this recipe for a traditional New England dish that gets its flavor from the lemon sauce.

for the pudding:
1/3 cup (2/3 stick) sweet butter
1/2 cup sugar
1 egg, beaten
1-1/2 cups flour
1-1/2 teaspoons baking powder
1/2 teaspoon salt
1/2 cup milk
1 teaspoon vanilla

for the sauce:
1/2 cup sugar
1 tablespoon cornstarch
1 teaspoon grated lemon peel
1 cup cold water
2 tablespoons sweet butter
2 tablespoons lemon juice
nutmeg to taste (optional)
1/2 cup raisins (optional)

For the pudding: Preheat the oven to 350 degrees. Cream together the butter and sugar and add the egg. Combine the dry ingredients and add them to the butter mixture alternately with the combined milk and vanilla. Pour into a buttered 9-inch-square cake pan. Bake for 30 minutes. Serve with the hot lemon sauce.

For the hot lemon sauce: Combine the first 4 ingredients in a saucepan. Cook for 5 minutes, stirring until thickened. Remove the sauce from the heat and add the butter and lemon juice, plus the nutmeg and/or raisins if you choose. Pour over slices of pudding. You may want to make a double batch of sauce; it's addictive.

Serves 9.

Leavitt Pudding

This bread pudding comes from the family lore of Charlotte Cox Thwing, a major participant in the Hawley bicentennial pageant (she's wearing a pink dress and a large bonnet in the painting on the cover of this book). Her relatives served it at Thanksgiving at least five generations back. Charlotte is a descendant of the infamous Parson Leavitt, a minister who (true to the ways of early New England churches) so alienated his congregation in Charlemont that they redrew their boundaries to place his house outside the town! She recalls as a child watching her uncles, all clergymen, help "in determining whether the 'hard sauce' had sufficient flavoring." You may also serve this pudding with a basic butter-and-sugar hard sauce, using 1 teaspoon of vanilla instead of the rum.

for the pudding:
softened sweet butter as needed for the bread and baking dish
1 cup red currant jelly
1 loaf firm white bread
1 cup sugar
1 teaspoon cinnamon
1/2 teaspoon nutmeg
1 cup (plus) raisins
8 eggs
1-1/2 teaspoons vanilla
1/2 teaspoon salt
4 to 6 cups milk

for the hard sauce:
1 cup (2 sticks) sweet butter, at room temperature
3-1/3 cups confectioner's sugar
1/4 teaspoon cinnamon
1/4 teaspoon nutmeg
1 dash salt
1 tablespoon rum

To make the pudding: Butter a large round baking dish. For each layer, spread butter and jelly on 3 slices of bread. Cut off the crusts. Cut and fit the bread into the bottom of the baking dish. Combine the sugar and spices, and sprinkle a layer of that combination over the bread. Cover with about 1/4 of the raisins. Repeat this process until the dish is full—about 4 layers when pressed down. Beat the eggs slightly, and add the vanilla and salt. Add this mixture to 4 cups of the milk. Pour it over the bread little by little until the custard is absorbed. If the dish is not filled to the brim, add extra milk to fill it. Place the dish in a shallow pan of water, and bake in a low (175-degree) oven for 6 to 8 hours or even a bit longer. Serve warm.

For the hard sauce: Cream the butter until soft and smooth. Add the other ingredients. The mixture should be fairly stiff when finished. Press it into a small dish, and refrigerate it overnight before serving it with the pudding.

Serves 10 to 12 generously.

A Final Digression: In Aunt Jerusha's Kitchen

One of my favorite characters in the Hawley Bicentennial Pageant, in which the pudding contest was reenacted, was Jerusha King. This long-lived (1788-1882) townswoman of Hawley's early years was portrayed with humor and gusto by my mother in a scene set in 1820.

Jerusha King was a notable personage in Hawley. She was the town's earliest historian, recording such stories as the tale of Hawley's first Thanksgiving, in which her grandfather, Thomas King, participated. She also transcribed a number of early records that would otherwise be lost. She was a home-educated writer of light verse with a charming sense of humor. Her poem, "In Our Grandmother's Days," was printed in William Atkins' *History of Hawley*. And as a mother, grandmother, aunt, and neighbor, Jerusha King stood in the center of Hawley's social activity for most of the 19th century. As one obituary recalled, "She was possessed of a fine constitution, was active and industrious, and for many long years 'Aunt' Jerusha's hospitality was extended to friends. Her name was a household word and she was one of those town aunts who is a friend to everybody."

Just for fun, I set out to learn what sort of foods might have been served in Aunt Jerusha's well populated kitchen around the year 1820. I used a variety of sources, including the three histories of Hawley to date; Waverly Root and Richard de Rochemont's entertaining chronicle *Eating in America*; and the scholarly but useful study *Landscape and Material Life in Franklin County, Massachusetts, 1770-1860*, by J. Ritchie

Garrison. I also took advantage of my mother Jan's knowledge of antiques and of my own common sense and imagination.

What was 32-year-old Jerusha King's life like in 1820? She lived in a busy household headed by her husband, Ezra King. A King by birth and a King by marriage, Jerusha had actually married her half-uncle. (Presumably Hawley's dating pool was even more limited in 1806, when the pair wed, than it is today.)

The Kings had given birth to eight of their 12 children by 1820. These youngsters ranged in age from baby John, born in November 1819, to 14-year-old Hiram, born a month before his

parents' marriage. (Premarital pregnancy was a common occurrence in the new Republic.)

In contrast to the relatively seasonal routine of her agriculturalist husband, Jerusha's work around the farm would have consisted mostly of daily tasks like poultry and pig care; dairying; keeping an eye on the children; and creating and caring for clothes through spinning, weaving, sewing, and washing.

She also performed functions that depended on the season—cheesemaking early in the year, care of calves and piglets in spring, gardening and gathering of produce in warmer months, and slaughtering (or at least the processing of slaughtered animals) and cider making in the brisk months of autumn.

And, of course, she cooked daily–dishing up the substantial breakfasts, mid-day dinners, and simple suppers that characterized farm life in her day.

The materials she used for preparing and storing food were primitive by our standards. She cooked on an open hearth–a task that seems Herculean to anyone who tries it today!–and did her best to preserve comestibles. She made use of covered crocks, sun and oven drying, and ice stored from the winter to keep foods fresh as long as possible. Glass was rare, and food processing as we know it had not yet been invented.

Like many Americans of her day, she probably served a great deal of salt meat, but fresh meat was available, too. Cooks in 1820 dished up pork, beef, lamb, veal, and poultry–plus freshly caught game and fish. Aunt Jerusha's cooking drew on a wide variety of vegetables, which she ate fairly quickly or stored as best she could, in her root cellar or in pickles and relishes.

According to Garrison's book, at least 26 varieties of seeds were available for sale locally in 1820. These included produce that kept well–like fresh or dried beans, peas, carrots, cabbages, herbs, corn, and parsnips–but also seasonal vegetables and fruits such as melons, endive, asparagus, and tomatoes.

The Kings' one-acre orchard also provided fruits to be eaten fresh, stored, and transformed into preserves, beverages, and edible leathers. Jerusha clearly knew, better than we do today, the thrill of greeting seasonal fruits one by one as the summer lengthened–and the chore of preserving those same fruits in bulk as the winter loomed.

She probably baked a great many pies to give her hardworking family members much needed calories. In all likelihood, however, she produced fewer cakes than today's farm cooks, relying instead on the all-purpose pudding for many desserts and savories.

As her poem indicates, Jerusha had little access to white flour and worked mostly with corn and rye in her breads and pastries. With no commercial yeast and no baking powder, she had to rely on baking soda and home-maintained cultures to make her baked goods rise. And with limited white sugar available, she generally used honey and maple products as sweeteners. The Hasty Pudding to which she refers in the poem is typical of her repertoire; a quick variant on Indian Pudding, it is made by sweetening cornmeal mush with maple syrup and throwing in spices and fresh or dried fruits.

Jerusha and her family undoubtedly produced butter, eggs, and cheese on their farm and brewed or stewed such beverages as cider, beer, and fruit wines for home use. The Kings probably went to a store in the lowlands for coffee, tea, malt (for beer making), sugar, molasses, fancier wines, and spices–exchanging butter, cheese, and/or lumber from their homestead for these products.

They also probably purchased the majority of the dishes on which they ate. These were most likely red ware, an attractive form of pottery in vogue in the early 19th century but later abandoned as its red color came from lead, which ultimately poisoned many of its users. Pewter and treen ware (wooden plates and bowls, named for the trees that produced them) were also common in kitchen's like Jerusha's. The Kings may have dined off more elegant, imported Staffordshire pottery on formal occasions when Jerusha provided the rich hospitality for which she was known.

We don't know what Aunt Jerusha King looked like, and the house she shared with her husband and children is lost to us, replaced long ago by brush and trees in the Hawley State Forest. Nevertheless, we can still appreciate her lively voice in the poem that follows, and we can simulate the taste of her hearth-warmed home by preparing foods similar to those she knew. The dandelion wine (see page 46) and the Indian pudding (see page 153) in this book are excellent examples with which to start.

Lorelei Lee in the Garden

In Our Grandmother's Days
by Jerusha King, 1878

This poem is reprinted from William Giles Atkins' History of Hawley (1887). Jerusha King's bearded stereotype of Jewish men is typical of her generation.

I think that you would like to know
How things were done long years ago,
And I have lived to eighty-four
And I can tell what people wore.

Men wore felt hats of coarsest wool,
Boys wore buff caps to church and school,
The ladies they wore pasteboard hats,
Their muffs were made of skins of cats.

Men's clothes were made of wool and flax;
They washed and shaved as neat as wax,
They never looked like Esau's race,
With hair that covered all their face.

The ladies they all dressed plain and neat,
In everything from head to feet;
They never wore the thing they call
A bustle or a waterfall.

We spun and wove the cloth to wear,
Or worked out in the open air.
We pulled the flax and loaded hay,
And helped to stow it all away.

To card and spin, and knit and sew,
We learned; all kinds of house-work, too.
To wash and bake, and churn and brew,
And get up a good dinner, too.

We did not live on pie and cake,
As 'tis the fashion now;
Our suppers, then, we did not take
Till we had milked the cow.

And then we had our milk and bread,
Our porridge made of beans, instead;
Or hasty pudding, warm and sweet,
And sometimes we had fish or meat.

Our bread was made of corn and rye,
Bolted it made our crusts for pie.
We always had enough to eat,
But very seldom any wheat.

The Bridge at Year's End

Index

Acorn Squash, Maple Baked 112

Alan's Cider Syrup Roasted Root Vegetables with
    Orange Cardamom Dressing 84

Alice's Bread 91

Appetizers
  Esty's Secret Smoked Lox 68
  Jane's Tex-Mex Turnovers 69
  Marge's Tex-Mex Dip 82

Apple Cider Chicken 109

Apple Pie à la Française 149

Apple Pound Cake 105

Applesauce Cake, Lena LaBelle's 106

Arnie's Squash Latkes 90

Asparagus à la Bambi 139

Asparagus Pudding 155

Aunt Fox's Carrot Soufflé 71

Aunt Lena's Bread-and-Butter Pickles 136

Aunt Lizzie's Ginger Drink 47

Aunt Lura's Cranberry Chutney 129

Baked Beans, Maple Pea 17

Banana Cake, Louise's 13

Basil or Rosemary Jelly 124

Beef
  Florette's Beef in Horseradish Sauce 6
  Guinness Pot Roast 87
  Hamburger Stroganoff 135
  Helen's Roast-Beef Salad 95
  Sate (Satay) from Indonesia 70
  Shepherd's Pie 143
  Tamale Pie 145

Beets, Harvard 47

Beets, Maple Pickled 19

Berry Vinegar 125

Best Cookies, The 93

Beverages
  Aunt Lizzie's Ginger Drink 47
  Florette's Rhubarb Tea 41
  Merry Lion MTC Punch 92
  Mohawk Trail Concerts Punch 92
  Raspberry Cordial 60
  Shelburne Falls Coffee Roasters' Iced Latte 81

Bill Shea's Omelettes 94

Black-Bean Soup, Mother's 85

Black-Bottom Cupcakes 29

Blackberry Pudding 62

Blackberry Sally Lunn 62

Blueberry Buckwheat Pancakes, The Copper
    Angel's 86

Blueberry Butter 61

Blueberry Crisp 61

Blueberry Muffins 60

Bob Stone's Fullerville Pie Crust 147

Bobbie's Chicken and Lemon 72

Bread Puddings
  Eric Carle's Bread Pudding 157
  Leavitt Pudding 161

Breads, Biscuits, and Muffins
  Alice's Bread 91
  Blueberry Muffins 60
  Elaine's Swedish Oatmeal Bread 12
  Graham Biscuits 11
  Janice Shea's Zucchini Bread 117
  Judy's Pumpkin Bread 133
  Pine Brook Farm Dill Bread 49
  Quick Graham Bread 20

Breads, Biscuits, and Muffins, *continued*
  Rhubarb Bread 38
  Sarah's Sweet Scones 79
  Shelburne Falls Coffee Roasters' Mixed-Berry
      Scones 63
  Summer Cheddar Muffins 118
Broccoli Salad 10
Brownies and Bars
  Maple Squares 22
  Rhubarb Bars 39
  Zucchinipalooza Zucchini Spice Brownies 115
Buckeyes 27
Butternut Squash, Maple-Glazed 117

Cabbage Potato Soup, Donovan 108
Cakes and Cupcakes
  Apple Pound Cake 105
  Black-Bottom Cupcakes 29
  Blackberry Sally Lunn 62
  Dot's Sour Cream Coffee Cake 101
  Froggie Chocolate Cake 138
  Gingerbread Ring Cake 101
  Jam Dandy 132
  Lena LaBelle's Applesauce Cake 106
  Louise's Banana Cake 13
  Strawberry Cake 58
  Teri's Pumpkin Cake 119
  Viennese Chocolate Cherry Cake 73
  Zucchini Chocolate Cake 114
Canadian Shepherd's Pie 144
Candies and Sweets
  Buckeyes 27
  Cream Candy 28
  Hawley Snowballs 30
  Maple Candy Corn 22

Penuche 27
Zagreb Turtles and Hawley Tortoises 32
Carrot Soufflé, Aunt Fox's 71
Charlemont Inn's Cider Maple Dumplings, The
    23
Cheese
  Goat Cheese à la Blue Heron Farm 52
  Peter's Stilton-Leek Tart 146
Chicken
  Apple Cider Chicken 109
  Bobbie's Chicken and Lemon 72
  Canadian Shepherd's Pie 144
  Chicken with Raspberry Vinegar 127
  Cousin Nancy's Chicken Soup 134
  I Got Rhubarb! 37
  Jan Weisblat's Indian Chicken Curry 71
  Jane's Tex-Mex Turnovers 69
  Keenan Cuisine Chicken Pot Pie 142
  Yankee Doodle Days White Chili 8
Chicken with Raspberry Vinegar 127
Chili, Yankee Doodle Days White 8
Chocolate Pudding 156
Colcannon 104
Cold Zucchini Soup 112
Cookies
  Best Cookies, The 93
  Gum-Drop Cookies 30
  Kate's Fantastic Ginger Snaps 33
  McCusker's Harvest Moon Cookies 80
  Molasses Cookies 33
  Pat's Prizewinning Oatmeal-Raisin Cookies
      103
Copper Angel's Sunday Brunch Blueberry
    Buckwheat Pancakes, The 86

Corn
  Corn Casserole 135
  Corn Pudding 153
  Pesto Butter for Sweet Corn 50
  Winter Corn and Tomato Soup 6
Cornmeal
  Indian Pudding 153
  Tamale Pie 145
Cottage Pudding 160
Cousin Nancy's Chicken Soup 134
Cranberries
  Aunt Lura's Cranberry Chutney 129
  McCusker's Harvest Moon Cookies 80
  Mock Cherry Pie 148
  Nancy Dole's Cranberry Relish 81
  Nantucket Cranberry Pie 147
Cream Candy 28
Cream-Cheese Frosting 114
Crystallized Violets and Johnny Jump-Ups 137
Curry, Jan Weisblat's Indian Chicken 71

Dandelion Wine, Rachel Kelley's 46
Deacon Porter's Hat 158
Dill Bread, Pine Brook Farm 49
Donovan Baby Red Potato Salad 102
Donovan Cabbage Potato Soup 108
Dot Clark's Doughnuts 100
Dot's Sour Cream Coffee Cake 101
Dragon Brook Farm Peach-Ginger Chutney 137

Elaine's Swedish Oatmeal Bread 12
Elsa Bakalar's Garden-Party Trifle 51
Eric Carle's Bread Pudding 157
Esty's Secret Smoked Lox 68

Florette's Beef in Horseradish Sauce 6
Florette's Rhubarb Tea 41
Flowers, Edible
  Crystallized Violets and Johnny Jump-Ups 137
Fresh Tomato Salad 72
Fritters, Rhubarb 43
Froggie Chocolate Cake 138
Frostings and Hard Sauces
  Cream-Cheese Frosting 114
  Great Grandmother Schneider's Chocolate
      Frosting 138
  Hard Sauce for Deacon Porter's Hat 159
  Teri's Secret Raisin Frosting 119
Fruit Crisps
  Blueberry Crisp 61
  Rhubarb Crisp 38
Fudge Sauce, Merry Lion Hot 82

Ginger Drink, Aunt Lizzie's 47
Ginger Snaps, Kate's Fantastic 33
Gingerbread Ring Cake 101
Glazed Pecans 31
Goat Cheese à la Blue Heron Farm 52
Graham Biscuits 11
Graham Bread, Quick 20
Grandmother Parker's Cracker Pudding 154
Great Grandmother Schneider's Chocolate
    Frosting 138
Guinness Pot Roast 87
Gum-Drop Cookies 30

Hamburger Stroganoff 135
Hard Sauce for Deacon Porter's Hat 159
Harvard Beets 47

Hawley Snowballs 30
Hawley Torte 74
Helen's Balsamic Vinegar Dressing 95
Helen's Roast-Beef Salad 95
Herbal Products
    Basil or Rosemary Jelly 124
    Herbal Vinegar 126
    Mint Syrup 126
Horseradish Jelly 129
Horseradish Sauce, Florette's Beef in 6

I Got Rhubarb! 37
Indian Pudding 153

Jam Dandy 132
Jams and Jellies
    About Processing 123
    Basil or Rosemary Jelly 124
    Blueberry Butter 61
    Horseradish Jelly 129
    Pepper Jelly 122
    Strawberry-Rhubarb Jam 59
Jan Weisblat's Indian Chicken Curry 71
Jan's Cordon Bleu Onion Soup 7
Jane's Tex-Mex Turnovers 69
Janice Shea's Zucchini Bread 117
Judy's Pumpkin Bread 133

Kate's Fantastic Ginger Snaps 33
Keenan Cuisine Chicken Pot Pie 142
Lamb
    Shepherd's Pie 143
Latte, Shelburne Falls Coffee Roasters Iced 81
Leavitt Pudding 161
Lena LaBelle's Applesauce Cake 106

Lime Jell-O Marshmallow Cottage Cheese
    SURPRISE! 97
Liza's Mustard 128
Louise's Banana Cake 13

Maple-Baked Acorn Squash 112
Maple-Balsamic Vinaigrette 19
Maple-Glazed Butternut Squash 117
Maple Candy Corn 22
Maple House Pizza Crust 145
Maple Pea Baked Beans 17
Maple Pickled Beets 19
Maple Recipes, Miscellaneous
    Charlemont Inn's Cider-Maple Dumplings, The
      23
    Quick Graham Bread 20
    Pudding Chômeur 21
    Vermont Pork Chops 18
Maple Red Cabbage 18
Maple Squares 22
Marge's Tex-Mex Dip 82
McCusker's Harvest Moon Cookies 80
Merry Lion Hot Fudge Sauce 82
Merry Lion MTC Punch 92
Merry Lion Sweet-and-Sour Vinaigrette 127
Mint Syrup 126
Mock Cherry Pie 148
Mohawk Trail Concerts Punch 92
Molasses Cookies 33
Mother's Black Bean Soup With (or Without)
    Chicken 85
Mustard, Liza's 128
Mustard Sauce Inspired by Mary Dole, A 54
My Grandmother's Squash Pie 148

Nancy Dole's Cranberry Relish 81
Nantucket Cranberry Pie 147
Norton Juster's Oatmeal Pie 96
Nuts
  Glazed Pecans 31

Oatmeal Bread, Elaine's Swedish 12
Oatmeal Pie, Norton Juster's 96
Oatmeal-Raisin Cookies, Pat's Prizewinning 103
Omelettes, Bill Shea's 94
Onion Soup, Jan's Cordon Blue 7

Pancakes
  Arnie's Squash Latkes 90
  The Copper Angel's Sunday Brunch Blueberry
    Buckwheat Pancakes 86
Pastas and Pasta Sauces
  Round Garden Pasta Salad 53
  Uncle Jack's Sausage and Peppers 9
Pat's Prizewinning Oatmeal-Raisin Cookies 103
Pat's Risotto Primavera 50
Peanut Sauce 70
Pecans, Glazed 31
Penuche 27
Pepper Jelly 122
Pesto Butter for Sweet Corn 50
Peter's Stilton-Leek Tart 146
Pickles, Relishes, and Chutneys
  About Processing 123
  Aunt Lena's Bread-and-Butter Pickles 136
  Aunt Lura's Cranberry Chutney 129
  Dragon Brook Farm Peach-Ginger Chutney
    137
  Maple Pickled Beets 19
  Nancy Dole's Cranberry Relish 81

Pudding Hollow Emilianna Relish 116
Pie Crust, Bob Stone's Fullerville 147
Pies
  Apple Pie à la Française 149
  Canadian Shepherd's Pie 144
  Keenan Cuisine Chicken Pot Pie 142
  Mock Cherry Pie 148
  My Grandmother's Squash Pie 148
  Nantucket Cranberry Pie 147
  Norton Juster's Oatmeal Pie 96
  Peter's Stilton-Leek Tart 146
  Rhubarb Custard Pie 40
  Rhubarb Pie 40
  Shepherd's Pie 143
  Tamale Pie 145
Pine Brook Farm Dill Bread 49
Pizza Crust, Maple House 145
Polly's Pumpkin Soup 113
Popcorn Balls
  Hawley Snowballs 30
Pork Chops, Vermont 18
Potatoes
  Colcannon 104
  Donovan Baby Red Potato Salad 102
  Donovan Cabbage Potato Soup 108
Processing, About 123
Pudding Chômeur 21
Pudding Hollow Emilianna Relish 116
Puddings
  Asparagus Pudding 155
  Blackberry Pudding 62
  Chocolate Pudding 156
  Corn Pudding 153
  Cottage Pudding 160
  Deacon Porter's Hat 158

Puddings, *continued*
  Eric Carle's Bread Pudding 157
  Grandmother Parker's Cracker Pudding 154
  Indian Pudding 153
  Leavitt Pudding 161
  Pudding Chômeur 21
  Strawberry Pudding 156
Pumpkin
  Judy's Pumpkin Bread 133
  My Grandmother's Squash Pie 148
  Polly's Pumpkin Soup 113
  Teri's Pumpkin Cake 119
Punch, Merry Lion MTC 92
Punch, Mohawk Trail Concerts 92

Quick Graham Bread 20

Rachel Kelley's Dandelion Wine 46
Raspberries with Chocolate Chantilly 59
Raspberry Cordial 60
Raspberry Vinegar, Chicken with 127
Red Cabbage, Maple 18
Rhubarb, Harvesting and Preparing 36
Rhubarb, I Got! 37
Rhubarb, Stewed 37
Rhubarb Bars 39
Rhubarb Bread 38
Rhubarb Crisp 38
Rhubarb Custard Pie 40
Rhubarb Fool, Ruth's 90
Rhubarb Fritters 43
Rhubarb Pie 40
Rhubarb Tea, Florette's 41
Rhubarb Wine 42
Risotto Primavera, Pat's 50

Rosemary
  Basil or Rosemary Jelly 124
Round Garden Pasta Salad 53
Ruth's Rhubarb Fool 90

Salads and Salad Dressings
  Broccoli Salad 10
  Donovan Baby Red Potato Salad 102
  Fresh Tomato Salad 72
  Helen's Balsamic Vinegar Dressing 95
  Helen's Roast-Beef Salad 95
  Maple-Balsamic Vinaigrette 19
  Merry Lion Sweet-and-Sour Vinaigrette 127
  Round Garden Pasta Salad 53
  Spinach Salad 10
  Uncle Abe's Orange and Onion Salad 68
Salmon
  Esty's Secret Smoked Lox 68
Sarah's Sweet Scones 79
Sate (Satay) from Indonesia 70
Sausage and Peppers, Uncle Jack's 9
Shelburne Falls Coffee Roasters' Iced Latte 81
Shelburne Falls Coffee Roasters' Mixed-Berry
    Scones 63
Shepherd's Pie 143
Shepherd's Pie, Canadian 144
Soups
  Cold Zucchini Soup 112
  Cousin Nancy's Chicken Soup 134
  Donovan Cabbage Potato Soup 108
  Jan's Cordon Bleu Onion Soup 7
  Mother's Black Bean Soup 85
  Polly's Pumpkin Soup 113
  Winter Corn and Tomato Soup 6
Spinach Salad 10

Squash Latkes, Arnie's 90
Squash Pie, My Grandmother's 148
Stewed Rhubarb 37
Stews and Pot Roasts
    Florette's Beef in Horseradish Sauce 6
    Guinness Pot Roast 87
Strawberry Cake 58
Strawberry Pudding 156
Strawberry-Rhubarb Jam 59
Summer Cheddar Muffins 118
Summer Squash
    Arnie's Squash Latkes 90
Swedish Oatmeal Bread, Elaine's 12

Tamale Pie 145
Tea, Florette's Rhubarb 41
Teri's Pumpkin Cake 119
Teri's Secret Raisin Frosting 119
Tomato Salad, Fresh 72
Tomato Soup, Winter Corn and 6
Trifle, Elsa Bakalar's Garden-Party 51
Turtles, Zagreb and Hawley Tortoises 32

Uncle Abe's Orange and Onion Salad 68
Uncle Jack's Sausage and Peppers 9

Vegetable Dishes
    Alan's Cider Syrup Roasted Root Vegetables
        with Orange Cardamom Dressing 84
    Asparagus à la Bambi 139
    Asparagus Pudding 155
    Aunt Fox's Carrot Soufflé 71
    Colcannon 104
    Corn Casserole 135
    Harvard Beets 47

Maple-Baked Acorn Squash 112
Maple-Glazed Butternut Squash 117
Maple Pickled Beets 19
Maple Red Cabbage 18
Peter's Stilton-Leek Tart 146
Round Garden Pasta Salad 53
Vermont Pork Chops 18
Viennese Chocolate Cherry Cake 73
Vinegars
    Berry Vinegar 125
    Herbal Vinegar 126

Wines
    Rachel Kelley's Dandelion Wine 46
    Rhubarb Wine 42
Winter Corn and Tomato Soup 6

Yankee Doodle Days White Chili 8

Zagreb Turtles and Hawley Tortoises 32
Zucchini
    Cold Zucchini Soup 112
    Janice Shea's Zucchini Bread 117
    Pudding Hollow Emilianna Relish 116
    Summer Cheddar Muffins 118
    Zucchini Chocolate Cake 114
    Zucchinipalooza Zucchini Spice Brownies 115

Looking for Paintings

Judith Russell's daughter, Cara Morton, is trying to locate all of her mother's art. If you have or know of any of Judy's painted works, or if you would like to share your views about Judy's art, Pudding Hollow, or this cookbook, please contact the Merry Lion Press at the following address:

The Merry Lion Press
84 Middle Road
Hawley, MA 01339

413-339-4747
info@merrylion.com